DICTATORSHIP 101

# AUTHORITARIAN LEADERSHIP SKILLS FOR BEGINNERS

*How You Can Gain Dictatorial Power and
Rule the World!*

James R. Martin

Real Deal Press

Real Deal Press/J R Martin Media Inc
jrmar2039@gmail.com

www.jrmartinmedia.com


FIRST EDITION

Book Design/Editing/Layout, James R. Martin - Real Deal Press

Ordering Information:
Quantity sales. Special discounts are available on quantity purchases by corporations, associations, and others. For details, contact the "Special Sales Department" at the e-mail address above.

Dictatorship 101: Authoritarian Leadership Skills for Beginners
ISBN:    979-8-9930561-0-4

All photographs and illustrations in this book are used with permission and/or attribution where possible. The publisher assumes no responsibility for errors, omissions, or inaccuracies in the work. This is a satirical work of fiction. Any resemblance of characters to persons living or dead is purely coincidental. Historical characters are referenced.

082925-i

# Acknowledgments

Dictatorship 101: Authoritarian Leadership Skills for Beginners inspired by today's world. Totalitarian wannabes are emerging everywhere. Many stumble and cause chaos without achieving lasting power as dictators, strongmen, or strong women. Their frequent mistakes and patchwork destruction of democratic governments motivated us to create this satirical guide.

We figure there are plenty of books about what these morons are doing to destroy the world. So why not try to educate authoritarian hopefuls on the reality of what it takes to succeed? And the pain of failure.

Photography and illustration for this book have come from many sources. This book uses original photographs and illustrations and others from the public domain with attribution permission. Additional sources are noted. All rights are reserved for all photography and copyrighted with the book. Permission to use this book's photographs will be granted after a written request. Attribution to source and this book is required.

The author condemns all atrocities, genocides, inquisitions, pogroms, assassinations, racism, ethnic and gender discrimination, and all crimes against humanity committed by dictators, authoritarians, fascists, and all persons living or dead.

# Dedication

*This book is dedicated to Family, Friends, and especially to Aaron and Marissa, Hy and Claire, and all the special people in my world.*

About the Author

James R. Martin is an Emmy Award–winning writer, director, and educator whose work spans film, television, and publishing. His documentaries have won Emmy awards, received nominations, and earned other honors. His books on filmmaking and storytelling are widely used in classrooms worldwide. With 'Dictatorship 101,' Martin combines his keen sense of narrative storytelling with satire, blending history and humor in a witty guide to authoritarian power.

Other Books by James R. Martin:

- Create Documentary Films, Videos, and Multimedia 3rd Edition
- Documentary Directing and Storytelling
- Actuality Interviewing and Listening
- Listen, Learn, Share
- Office and Home Tai Chi with Yue Zhang (translator, writer, and editor of the English edition)
- The Shaolin Temple Story (translator, writer, and editor)
- Storytelling in the SEO Age
Fiction:
- Silhouettes and Shadows, "Humanity Follows the Earth, Earth Follows the Universe"

# Table of Contents

# Preface

Ever imagined being a dictator, basking in an endless spotlight, your name shining across every billboard from here to the moon, with a 50-foot hologram of you winking at rush-hour traffic? Dictatorship 101 serves as your guide to authoritarianism, from Mussolini's balcony rants to Nayib Bukele's crown-filtered swagger. This manual breaks down the playbook of power—winning voters, rewriting rules, silencing critics, and becoming an autocrat. However, beware: history's dictators, from Viktor Orbán's media control in Hungary to Nicolás Maduro's protest-suppressing tactics in Venezuela, leave behind trails of oppression, fear, and broken lives. Syria's ruins and Cambodia's killing fields shout out the cost of unchecked power, where statues fall and #CancelLeader trends.

The author disclaims all responsibility for coups, rebellions, ill-advised uniform choices, or hostile corporate takeovers branded as 'synergistic leadership.' If you finish this guide itching to declare yourself Supreme Leader, try commissioning a bronze bust of your cat wearing a tiny dictator's cap instead— far less likely to spark a revolution. Freedom and fairness win over self-awarded medals, so read on, aspiring autocrat, but tread lightly: absolute power comes with a guillotine's shadow.

*Authoritarians are already using the skills you are learning. The rest of the world is learning about them now too.*

# Introduction

Aspire to rule with an iron fist and a viral selfie? Inspired by Alexander the Great's conquests, Julius Caesar's toga-clad swagger, or Vladimir Putin's shirtless bravado, you might think, "Absolute power could fix everything." This guide shows you how to become a first-generation dictator by blending historical lessons (Hitler's propaganda, Stalin's purges, Pol Pot's genocide) with modern tactics (Trump's X rants, Bukele's social media flair, Maduro's election rigging). From charming voters to rewriting history, it's a playbook for power—wrapped in a bit of satiric humor. The path is full of bad optics and worse outcomes—think Nero's fiddle, Ceaușescu's execution, or Gaddafi's desert demise. Before you nod eagerly, grab a history book or rethink your goals. The risks? Angry mobs, sanctions, or a one-way ticket to obscurity. Ready for your autocratic audition? Let's dive in. Keep your elbows at the ready.

**Pro Tip**: Practice your "benevolent tyrant" stare in the mirror. If your goldfish salutes, you're ready to roll. Think about how you can take advantage of the many opportunities for advancement that appear in each chapter.

**Authoritarian:** *Demanding complete obedience and refusing to allow individuals the freedom to act as they wish. It refers to an authoritarian regime, dictatorship, government, or ruler.*

**Dictator:** *A leader with total power over a country or group, often acting without the limits of a constitution or legal restrictions. Dictatorships lack checks and balances, suppress opposition, and control key parts of society like the media and courts.*

# FORWARD

## By Saddam Hussein

*(As channeled from the great beyond.)*

My fellow aspiring tyrants, comrades in ambition, and dreamers of iron-fisted glory, as I ponder from the spectral sands of eternity, where statues no longer stand and my once-mighty mustache no longer receives salutes, I write this for Dictatorship 101 with a heavy heart. Perhaps, if I had held this guide in my calloused hands during my reign, the Euphrates would still sing my praises, and my palaces would not echo with the footsteps of invaders and gunfire. I once led Iraq through thirty years of what I called "glorious history."

In my time, I thought ruling came naturally—an art of tanks, brutality, loyalty, bribes, and well-placed statues. I called our army's 82nd anniversary in 2003 a testament to "the great values and mission entrusted to our nation," a source of pride for the Mujahideen and freedom fighters. I shocked the world with my 1990 Kuwait gambit. I blamed "external enemies" like a pro, but there was no TikTok for my speeches, unlike now with Bukele, Orbán, or Putin. It took the world to stop me from taking Kuwait and its oil riches.

You must have a doctrine of faith, much like I once called Iraq's path—a source of pride for the Mujahideen of ambition and a reservoir of strategies for your children and grandchildren under autocracy. It is not just an isolated event but part of the broader power struggle, linked to the pursuits of Putin, Xi, and Kim, whose successes in 2025 mock my downfall. My dictatorship was a symbol of tyranny and corruption, but enemies aimed to topple my reign of terror by falsely claiming I possessed a nuclear bomb. I might have avoided the destruction of the Gulf War, escaped the noose, and kept my statues standing. Instead, I was hunted down, and my legacy was reduced to a spider hole.

Aspiring dictators, take note, you must have a shield against being dragged through the streets, losing your family and throne—whether in a palace or a corner office. But beware, even corporate dictators face #CancelCDO hashtags. Ignoring reality as I did could be risky, for the crowd that cheers your rise will welcome your exit.

Eternally yours in fascist spirit,

Saddam Hussein
*(From the afterlife, where Wi-Fi is terrible and statues are few).*

## *An Ongoing Story*

*Winding through Dictatorship 101 is an ongoing story about three individuals who choose to advance their careers with determination and often authoritarian ruthlessness. They move from ordinary jobs to new pursuits.*

Three ambitious people—Coach Rob Stevenson, Lawyer Margaret Miller, and Entrepreneur businessman Paul Stewart Johnson—climb the ladders of power in politics, business, and national ambition. Alongside the lessons of Dictatorship 101, their stories unfold chapter by chapter: campaigns fueled by charisma, boardrooms reshaped into fiefs, and rallies transformed into spectacles. Each character masters the textbook tactics—rewriting rules, silencing rivals, building monuments—while ignoring the cracks forming beneath them. It's a study of how authoritarian instincts thrive in familiar settings. The question isn't whether their rise will end, but how loudly they'll cheer if floor gives way.

# Chapter 1

## *Spotting Opportunities for Power*

*Control the story, headlines, and the applause. Bonus points if you also control the media.*

### Spotting Opportunities for Power

Authoritarian leaders often succeed in chaotic situations—such as economic collapse, social unrest, political divisions, or war. Remember, if these conditions aren't present, you can create them. Use your power and resources to instigate chaos or destabilize the economy. Modern "electoral autocrats" like Viktor Orbán (Hungary) or Recep Tayyip Erdoğan (Turkey) manipulate democratic systems to establish hybrid regimes that appear democratic but operate autocratically. Here's how to recognize your moment and capitalize on it like a pro.

### Crises as Springboards

Crises act as springboards to power because they push people to their limits, forcing them to face challenges and adapt quickly. These intense moments peel away superficial layers, exposing weaknesses that lead to insecurity and fear. The aspiring dictator can exploit these moments.

### Economic Distress

Orbán exploited Hungary's 2008 financial crisis, blaming socialists to secure a two-thirds majority in 2010, and rewrote the constitution by 2011 to strengthen Fidesz's power (NYTimes, "Hungary's Slide Toward Autocracy," 2012). Juan Perón addressed Argentina's economic issues in the 1940s, promising labor reforms to win the 1946 election (BBC, "Perón's Argentina," 2020)..

### Security Fears

Nayib Bukele won El Salvador's 2019 election, promising to fight gang violence, declaring a 2022 state of emergency that led to over 70,000 arrests by 2024, often without due process, drawing both praise and UN scrutiny (NPR, "Bukele's Crackdown," 2024). You can exploit issues like immigration, crime rates, and natural disasters to take control of cities. Blame and remove rivals from opposition parties.

### Political Discontent

Jair Bolsonaro capitalized on Brazil's 2018 anti-corruption sentiment by using WhatsApp to spread anti-elite messages and won despite praising the 1964–1985 dictatorship (Euronews, "Bolsonaro's Rise," 2018). Tunisia's Kais Saied used 2019's anti-elite sentiment to dissolve parliament by 2022 (Al Jazeera, "Saied's Power Grab," 2022).

### Social Polarization

Nicolás Maduro took power in Venezuela during the post-Chávez chaos in 2013, using falling oil prices to justify populist rule, with hyperinflation reaching 1,000,000% by 2018 (New Yorker, "Venezuela's Collapse," 2018).

### War or Instability

Idi Amin took control of Uganda during a 1971 coup amid ethnic tensions, ruling through fear until 1979 (BBC, "Amin's Reign," 2003). Bashar al-Assad suppressed the 2011 Arab Spring protests, which led to Syria's civil war and over 500,000 deaths (UN, "Syria Conflict," 2024). Pol Pot's 1975 Khmer Rouge takeover took advantage of Cambodia's civil war, resulting in 1.7 million deaths (BBC, "Khmer Rouge," 2020).

### Personal Development

To start your political career, you're running for a seat on the local school board. You learn that a new math textbook is being introduced. Review the book to see if there's anything you can claim is controversial about the author's approach to Algebra, or perhaps about the author herself—campaign to investigate this urgent controversy if elected. There is a serious threat to students' learning from this dangerous form of Algebra.

### Modern Autocrats' Playbook
*Shared tactics define the game:*

### Exploit crises

If there isn't a crisis, create one. It doesn't need to be real—just make something up. Promise bold fixes, like Erdoğan's post-2016 coup purges targeting 100,000 "traitors" (CRD, "Turkey's Purge," 2017). Suharto's 1965 Indonesian coup capitalized on anti-communist fears, leading to up to 1 million deaths (BBC, "Suharto's Legacy," 2008). Claim elections are rigged by mail-in voting and voting machines. Then launch a campaign against illegal voting, (US, Trump Regime, 2025).

### Control Institutions

Rewrite constitutions (Hungary), stack courts (El Salvador), or establish loyal bodies (Venezuela's 2017 parallel legislature). Yoweri Museveni's removal of the 2005 term limit in Uganda has solidified his rule since 1986 (Human Rights Watch, "Museveni's Grip," 2024). In many countries, the national democratic constitution is not strongly protected or does not require ratification, as is the case in the United States. In long-standing constitutional democracies, authoritarian leaders often need the courts' support to ignore constitutional precedents. Filling courts with supporters can help influence the outcome of laws.

## BASIC ASPECTS OF AUTHORITARIAN DICTATOR FEARMONGERING

(AS TAUGHT IN THE UNOFFICIAL "DICTATORSHIP 101" CRASH COURSE)

| ASPECT | HOW IT WORKS | WHY IT'S EFFECTIVE | CLASSIC EXAMPLE |
|---|---|---|---|
| INVENT AN EXTERNAL ENEMY | Pick a foreign country, group, or ideology to demonize. Constantly portray them as as plotting your downfall. | Unites population under you as their "protector." | Cold War anti-communist hysteria: "Foreign meddling" claims |
| INTERNAL THREAT SCAPEGOAT | Target an internal minority, dissidents, or political rivals. Accuse them of subversion. | Distracts from your failures and consolidates majority support | "Without me, the country will fall apart!" speeches "Without me the country will fall apart!" speeches |
| DOOMSDAY PROPHECIES | Warn of impending chaos, economic collapse, or moral decay if you lose power. | Creates dependency — you become the "only" savior | Dictators declaring emergency powers after mysterious "incidents." |
| CONTROLLED CRISES | Manufacture or exaggerate threats (crime waves, epidemics, shortages) to d swoop in to "solve" them. | Turns you into the heroic problem-solver | "If you're not with us, you're against us" Pyongyang military parades. Cold War propaganda films |
| DEMONIZE DISSENT | Equate criticism with treason or aiding the enemy | Makes fear tangible and memorable | Keeps everyone anxious and obedient |

### Fearmongering

Create an external enemy, find an internal scapegoat, invent doomsday prophecies, manufacture crises, demonize dissenters and protesters, and invent enemies. Exaggerate threats, such as Augusto Pinochet's anti-communist purges in 1970s Chile, which led to 3,000 deaths (Amnesty International, "Chile's Dictatorship," 2020).

### Populist Rhetoric

Populist rhetoric is a communication style used by many authoritarian politicians, portraying themselves as defenders of the common people against out-of-touch liberals, the so-called elite or others. They simplify complex issues to

## KEY CHARACTERISTICS OF POPULIST RHETORIC

**US VS. THEM**
Populist rhetoric divides society into "the people" (good, ordinary citizens) and "the elite" (corrupt, self-serving). This fosters a shared sense of identity and grievance among the "people."

**SIMPLIFICATION**
Complex issues are presented in a straigrhtforwared and easily understandable way, often at the expense of nuance and complexity.

**EMOTIONAL APPEAL**
Populist rhetoric heavily relies on emotional language and appeals to anger, frustration towards the "elite."

**ANTI-ESTABLISHMENT SENTIMENT**
It often shows distrust or outright hostility toward established institutions, political parties, and the mdia.

**DIRECT DEMOCRACY**
Populists might support direct democracy methods, such as referendums, to avoid what they believe are corrupt or inefficient representative systems

**MORAL FRAMING**
The rhetoric often fames political issues in terms of morality, good versus evil, with the populist leader representing the virtuous side

create a narrative of "us versus them." The approach includes Us vs. Them, Simplification, Emotional Appeal, Anti-establishment Sentiment, Direct Democracy, Moral Framing, and Charismatic Leadership. This strategy aims to gather support by exploiting feelings of grievance and dissatisfaction with the current political system. It often involves oversimplifying complex issues, constructing a narrative of "us versus them," and appealing to emotions and popular sentiment.

### *Dominate Media*

Controlling broadcast and cable TV, radio, the internet, and social media is essential for spreading propaganda and misinformation without opposition. This can be achieved by purchasing media outlets (Turkey), using social media (Brazil), or banning critics (Venezuela). Thailand's Prayut Chan-o-cha censored media after the 2014 coup (Amnesty International, "Thailand's Coup," 2020). Constant lawsuits are also frequently filed against the media (US, 2025 Trump Regime). Control can also be maintained with the support of oligarchs who own large media groups.

## Case Studies

**Viktor Orbán** (Hungary): An anti-communist speech in 1989 launched his fame. After 2008, he blamed socialists and won in 2010. Fidesz gerrymandered districts, controlled 90% of the media by 2022, and hosted CPAC to inspire populists like Trump. As of 2025, EU funding cuts threaten his support, but his grip remains strong (Journal of Democracy, "How Orbán Wins," 2019).

**Recep Tayyip Erdoğan (Turkey):** Served as Prime Minister from 2003 to 2014 and as President from 2014 to now. Erdoğan shifted from a reformer to an autocrat after the 2013 Gezi protests. His response to the 2016 coup resulted in the purge of 100,000 judges, teachers, and journalists, and by 2025, 90% of the media was government-controlled (GMF, "Turkey's Authoritarianism," 2020). Denying inflation fuels unrest, but loyalists stay committed.

**Nayib Bukele (El Salvador):** A millennial former advertiser, Bukele won in 2019 with TikTok charisma, tackling gangs with 70,000 arrests by 2024. His court stacking allowed him to run for re-election in 2024, despite term limits, although UN scrutiny increased starting in 2025 (NPR, 2024).

**Nicolás Maduro (Venezuela):** Since 2013, Chávez's successor Maduro has banned opposition parties and manipulated the 2024 elections, leading to protests that loyalists suppressed. His 90% media control is similar to Orbán's, but the presence of 7 million emigrants and the threat of hyperinflation weaken his position (New Yorker, 2024).

**Rodrigo Duterte (Philippines**, 2016–2022): His "war on drugs" resulted in over 20,000 deaths, using fear and loyal police to sideline courts. Media harassment silenced critics like Maria Ressa, but term limits forced his departure (Human Rights Watch, "Duterte's Legacy," 2022)

**Kais Saied (Tunisia):** His "war on drugs" caused over 20,000 deaths, using fear and loyal police to sideline courts. Media harassment silenced critics like Maria Ressa, but term limits forced his departure (Human Rights Watch, "Duterte's Legacy," 2022).

**Yoweri Museveni (Uganda):** President since 1986, Museveni took power after the civil war, promising stability. His removal of the 2005 term limit and alleged election rigging in 2021 led to the imprisonment of rivals, including Bobi Wine. As of 2025, his control over media and the military continues to sustain his power (Human Rights Watch, 2024).

## Dictator Checklist

| Tactic | Example | Your Move |
|---|---|---|
| Exploit Crisis | Orbán's 2008 financial wave | Blame "elites" for a local scandal |
| Control Institutions | Bukele's court stacking | Rewrite condo board rules |
| Dominate Media | Erdoğan's outlet purchases | Start a #LeaderVibes X campaign |
| Populist Rhetoric | Bolsonaro's anti-corruption rants | Promise to "fix" slow Wi-Fi |
| Fear-Mongering | Pinochet's anti-communist purges | Warn of "traitors" at work |

**Pro Tip:** Check X for #SystemIsRigged trends. Promise to "solve" unemployment or crime—no details needed: Study Amin's 1971 coup or Suharto's 1965 massacre for chaos-exploiting flair. Promise millions of new jobs! Don't forget the "blame game." Find someone to blame for problems you claim you will solve.

**Personal Development:** Host a "crisis audition" at home. Declare a "dishwasher crisis" and demand loyalty from roommates. Accuse dissenters of "anti-household treason" and assign laundry duty: mimic Saied's 2021 emergency decrees or Museveni's election rigging for practice.

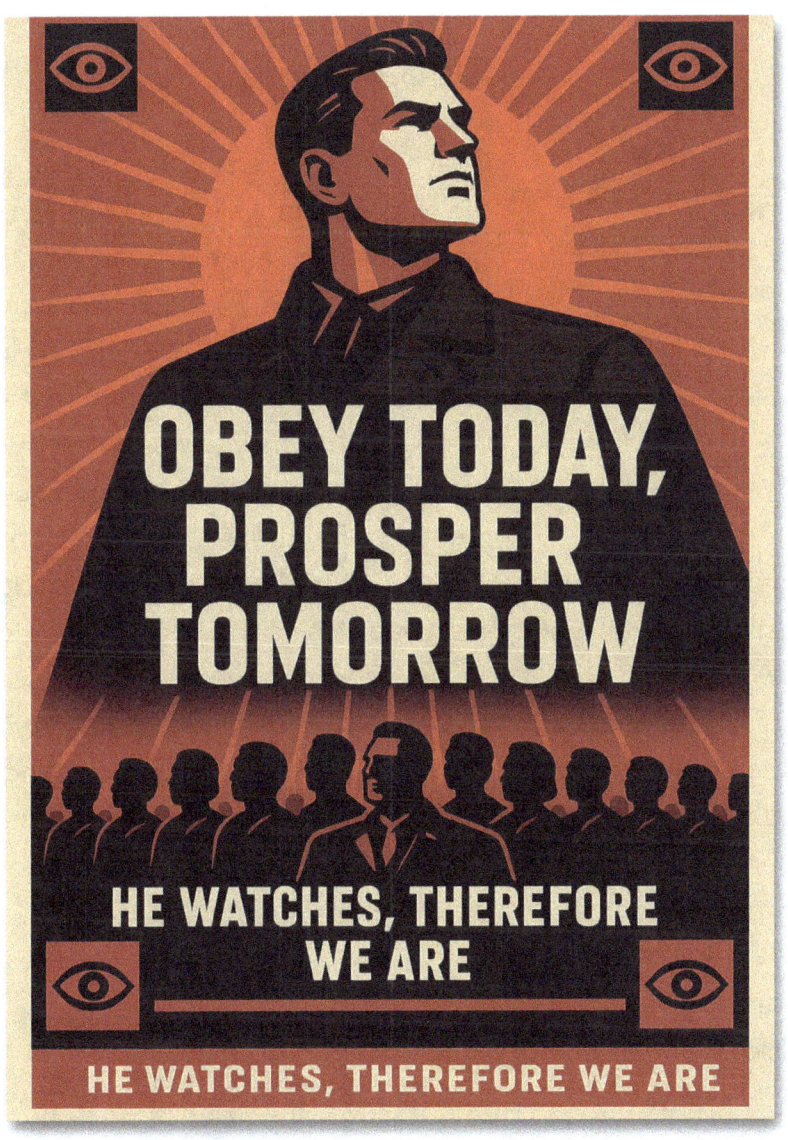

*My will is the nation's will. Any disagreement is treason.*

# An Ongoing Story

*Episode One*

Coach Rob Stevenson leaned against the cinder block wall of the high school gym, watching another disappointing season close with a slow clap from the town's mayor sitting in the parents' section. The team was bad, sure—but the mayor was worse. Old, complacent, barely awake at council meetings. Rob believed even he could do better. In fact, he would do better. When the town's budget crisis hit—layoffs, potholes, even closing the public pool—Rob saw his opening. At a coffee shop "town hall" (technically three guys at a Formica counter), he declared, "The mayor's mismanagement is killing community spirit. Even his sitting in the stands at my games is the kiss of death." By lunch, he'd lined up a retired sign painter, a box of old campaign buttons, and the vague confidence of a man with nothing to lose.

Sitting in her corner office, Margaret Miller pondered the partner track that always seemed just out of reach. The old boys' club at her firm was a fortress built on golf outings and bad whiskey. Then came the scandal: a rival partner was caught mishandling a major client's funds.

Margaret didn't see chaos—she saw a power vacuum. While HR drafted disciplinary memos, she was already at a discreet lunch with the company's largest client, subtly suggesting that their future might be better served with a more capable liaison. By the end of the week, she received an offer—not for partnership, but for a C-suite position at a major corporation. She didn't hesitate. Lawyers might draft the rules, but CFOs rewrite them

Paul Stewart Johnson's brunch was interrupted by a headline about a "fractured primary field" in the upcoming presidential race. His Brazilian trophy wife barely looked up from her salad when he shared his plan. "I'm going to run for President," he said. "You're already a billionaire and president of your corporations," she replied flatly. Paul smiled. "I'm going for the United States." He had been quietly funding attack ads against potential opponents for months— always through "independent" groups. His decades of selling cars and condos taught him that the best deals happen when the market is in chaos. And this election cycle? Pure chaos. Perfect for a man who could turn a handshake into a brand and a scandal into a marketing campaign.

To be continued.

**The Cult of Your Ego and Image**

Your face is everywhere—on billboards, coins, stadiums, parade floats, and school textbooks—making visibility a way to establish legitimacy.

**Signature Pose**  Make a bold gesture for public appearances, earning extra points if it appears heroic from any angle.

**Personal Logo** – A bold, simple symbol that can be used on everything from fighter jets to bread wrappers.

**Wardrobe as Weapon** – Uniforms represent discipline, suits stand for power, and track suits suggest "I could still run the country… literally."

**Hair as Policy** A distinctive hairstyle can outlast entire regimes in the public's memory.

**Ego Stagecraft**  Always arrive late so the crowd has time to soak in your absence.

**Own the Narrative** Craft a humble origin story or a grandiose one as long as you end up a Great Leader.

**Media Praise** Ensure interviews end with compliments from interviewers and celebrities.

**Reality Show Politics** Turn governance into daily spectacles, rallies, and dramatic announcements.

AUTHORITARIAN LEADERSHIP SKILLS FOR BEGINNERS

**EGO CULTIVATION CHECKLIST**

✓ PLASTER YOUR FACE EVERYWHERE
✓ CRAFT A SIGNATURE POSE
✓ DESIGN A PERSONAL LOGO
✓ WEAR A SPECIAL OUTFIT
✓ REWRITE YOUR BIOGRAPHY
✓ AWARD YOURSELF GRAND TITLES
✓ PROMOTE CONTRIVED CHARITY
✓ CHANGE ENEMIES REGULARLY
✓ NAME PLACES AFTER YOURSELF

# Chapter 2

## Cultivate Your Image and Ego

*"It is better to be feared than loved, if you cannot be both."*
*---Niccolò Machiavelli*

A dictator's ego demands its own time zone. Craft a persona that shouts "savior," blending style, swagger, and spectacle. Free your inner narcissist. Let people know how smart and brilliant you are with stories about your successes, real or imagined. Demean opponents as stupid and inferior to you in every way.

**Build Your Brand**

**Uniforms:** Think of Muammar Gaddafi's flamboyant capes, Augusto Pinochet's military regalia, or Putin's shirtless horseback rides. A slogan cap (Bukele's backwards cap) or a sharp suit (Atatürk's Western style) also works. Pol Pot's black pajamas projected revolutionary zeal (BBC, "Khmer Rouge," 2020).

**Titles:** Demand the 'Supreme Leader" at family dinners, like Kim Jong-un's god-king status or Idi Amin's "Conqueror of the British Empire." Award yourself medals for "breakfast bravery" or "email efficiency." Legacy," 2020). Suharto's Javanese stoicism masked his brutality from 1965 to 1998 (BBC, 2008).

**Public Persona:** Blend charisma and menace. Bolsonaro's "Trump of the Tropics" used X memes to rally Brazil's conservatives in 2018, while Mustafa Kemal Atatürk's tailored suits signaled modernity in 1920s Turkey (BBC, "Atatürk's Legacy," 2020). Suharto's Javanese stoicism masked his brutality from 1965 to 1998 (BBC, 2008).

**Branding:** Still in the wannabe dictator category, Donald J. Trump provides a prime example of branding everything with his name and face. Some things he owns, others he licenses his name for. Starting with Trump Tower hotels, casinos, and Trump Golf Courses, there have been many Trump-related ventures, including games, social media, magazines, TV game shows, films, books, a failed university, food and liquor products, and other projects. During his second term as president, he is aggressively trying to rename various entities, like the Kennedy Center, after himself. Let's not forget his private jet, marked with 'TRUMP' on the fuselage.

### Practice at Home
**Control Game Night:** *Rewrite the Monopoly rules so you always win. Call critics "board game traitors."*

**Mock Rallies***: Host a "movie night" but feature your campaign video. Call yourself "Minister of Popcorn."*

**Loyalty Tests***: Make friends salute your fridge selfie. Send skeptics to dish duty.*

### Historical and Modern Examples

**Saddam Hussein (Iraq)**: His medals and constant portraits made him appear invincible, like Kim's lapel pins. TV broadcasts praised his leadership during the 1980s Iran-Iraq War, hiding the 200,000 deaths (BBC, "Saddam's Image," 2003).

**Nayib Bukele (El Salvador)**: His 2024 TikTok videos, complete with crown filters, have helped him avoid constitutional bans and reinforce his "cool dictator" image despite 70,000 arrests (NPR, 2024).

**Jair Bolsonaro (Brazil):** His 2018 campaign memes and "savior" rhetoric echoed Trump. As of 2025, his posts about the coup trial call out "rigged judges," rallying loyalists (Euronews, "Bolsonaro's Trial," 2025).

**Idi Amin (Uganda):** His self-given titles and flashy uniforms made him a caricature, concealing up to 500,000 deaths. His removal from power in 1979 marked the end of his rule (BBC, 2003).

**Francisco Franco (Spain):** His somber uniforms and Catholic symbols projected stability after the 1936 Civil War, ruling until 1975 with 50,000 executions (BBC, "Franco's Spain," 2020).

**Pol Pot (Cambodia):** His Khmer Rouge rule from 1975 to 1979 used minimalist clothing and "Year Zero" rhetoric to erase history, killing 1.7 million (BBC, 2020).

**Pro Tip:** Post an X clip with #LeaderEnergy, showing how you "fix" a local pothole (or hire someone to fix it). Study Mussolini's balcony poses, Amin's medal-strewn jackets, or Suharto's quiet menace for flair.

**Personal Development:** Host a "Dictator Dress Rehearsal" party where guests must praise your outfit or face "fashion exile" (laundry duty). Mimic Bukele's TikTok swagger, Franco's stoic imagery, or Pol Pot's revolutionary austerity.

# An Ongoing Story

## Episode Two

His campaign kickoff wasn't quite Mussolini's balcony, but the folding chairs in the VFW hall were packed, and the homemade banner mostly spelled Rob Stevenson's name right. He wore his best suit and made sure to shake every hand twice. His nephew managed social media, flooding local feeds with photos of Rob looking thoughtful near potholes. When a supporter suggested a catchy slogan, Rob adopted it immediately: "Stevenson Saves the City." It didn't matter that he hadn't saved anything yet. The image was all about potential. Spotting a local photographer, he asked, "Can you take some good shots of me speaking and a couple of portraits? I'll remember your help."

Understanding that perception equals power came to Margaret instinctively. Within weeks at her new company, she curated a wardrobe: bold colors for board meetings and understated elegance for shareholder calls. She commissioned a professional headshot that radiated competence and authority. She instructed her new executive assistant, "to please always refer to her as 'Ms. Miller in public." A glossy industry magazine profile highlighting her "visionary leadership" solidified her status as a rising star in corporate finance. It was almost enough to make people forget she had only been there a month.

He didn't just enter politics; Paul arrived with a powerful presentation. His first rally had an LED backdrop displaying his name in gold, scrolling continuously. Every camera angle was tested for maximum impact. His campaign team filmed him shaking hands in diners, inspecting construction sites, and jogging—just enough to look athletic without breaking a sweat. "I'm going to rid this country of corruption and criminals," he told anyone who would listen. His social media feeds were a curated mix of patriotism, nostalgia, and just the right amount of outrage. The image of a strong, relatable leader was set. Whether it matched reality was beside the point.

To be continued.

"Good things come to those who know the pitch."

# Chapter 3

## Run for Office (Or Steal the Spotlight)

*History Remembers Winners.*

Your autocratic journey starts on the campaign trail—less emphasis on public service, more like a WWE show.

### Choose Your Issues

**Fear-Mongering:** Stir panic with phrases like "outsiders are stealing jobs" or "elites rigged the system." Joseph McCarthy's 1950s Red Scare accused enemies without evidence (History, "McCarthyism," 2020). Pinochet's anti-communist purges terrified Chileans (Amnesty International 2020

**Bold Promises:** *Vow to "restore greatness" or "ban slow elevators." Mussolini's "trains on time" myth or Chávez's oil-funded welfare impressed voters (BBC, "Chávez's Rise," 2002). Museveni's 1986 "stability" pledge gained Uganda's war-weary population (Human Rights Watch, 2024).*

**Dog Whistles:** Use coded messages, like Bolsonaro's anti-"communist" rants in 2018 or Trump's "MAGA" slogans (NYTimes, "Trump's Rhetoric," 2024). Prayut's "Thai values" after the 2014 coup silenced dissent (Amnesty International, 2020).

### If You are Rich

**Flash Cash:** Fund surges with fireworks, resembling Silvio Berlusconi's media-driven Italian campaigns (1994–2011). Brand hats, jets, or gold-plated toasters (BBC, "Berlusconi's Empire," 2011).

**Claim Outsider Status:** Say you are "unbuyable," despite your wealth. Complain about your yacht's taxes to "relate." Trump's 2015 escalator entrance and branded steaks screamed billionaire savior (CNN, "Trump's Business," 2016).
Example: Ferdinand Marcos employed wealth and martial law rhetoric in the 1970s, stealing $10 billion while projecting strength (Amnesty International, "Marcos's Legacy," 2020).

### If You are an Outsider

Play the Underdog: Draw on Juan Perón's humble Argentine roots or Hugo Chávez's military background, criticizing "corrupt elites" (BBC, 2002). Alexander Lukashenko's 1994 Belarus campaign portrayed him as a "man of the people" (BBC, "Lukashenko's Rise," 2020).

**Social Media Mastery:** Stream your coffee run live, starting with "As a regular guy…" Crowdsourcing funds suggests a "mystery donor." Kais Saied's 2019 Tunisian campaign used anti-elite videos to win (Al Jazeera, 2022).

**Example:** Mobutu Sese Seko's 1965 Congo coup capitalized on anti-colonial sentiment, calling himself "father of the nation" (BBC, 1997). Ismail Omar Guelleh's 1999 victory in Djibouti used port income to boost populism (Africa Report, "Guelleh's Rule," 2021).

**Pro Tip:** Leak a viral X video of you "saving" a stray dog (hire the dog). An alternative that might appeal to some supporters might be to shoot the stray dog, claiming it had fleas. Imitate Orbán's 2010 anti-EU campaign, Lukashenko's populist rallies, or Prayut's military-backed "stability" for a chaos-driven twist.

**Personal Development:** Study Bolsonaro's 2018 WhatsApp strategy, which sparked anti-elite outrage. As of 2025, his X posts still promote loyalty despite trial risks (Euronews, 2025). Use #NoElites to rally supporters or imitate Marcos's wealth-flaunting charisma or Guelleh's port-funded populism..

## *An Ongoing Story*

### *Episode Three*

Filling out the paperwork for Mayor, was approached with the same confidence Rob used to draw mock-up plays for the basketball team—leaning into a bit of improvisation and full of enthusiasm. His first debate was a performance. Rob delivered punchy one-liners, leaning on the microphone like a late-night comedian. He avoided specifics, promising to "fix what's broken" and "get this city moving again." "We need to stop the rise in crime in our town," he said. He hadn't heard of many crimes in the town of forty-four thousand people, but Mrs. Monihan reported she thought immigrant workers had stolen her pet cat, Julie. The incumbent tried to discuss policy, but

Rob cracked a joke about the mayor's pothole-filled streets. He said, "Yeah, my policy hurts every time I drive over a pothole." The audience erupted in laughter. The next day's headlines didn't mention the mayor's policy points—yet Rob's one-liner and smile were everywhere. "I'm going to need your support and help," Rob told his wife, Claire, a teacher, and their two teenage boys. Claire was a bit skeptical but fully supportive. They all agreed to attend campaign events as a family.

She had no plans to run for public office, but Margaret understood the influence of public perception. Her husband, a TV news producer, kept her updated on developments in the business world. When a rival CFO faltered during a televised earnings call, she volunteered to speak at the company's next major investor meeting. Her presentation was flawless: accurate data and memorable sound bites. Financial media quickly dubbed her "The Boardroom's Iron Lady." Investors appreciated her composure, while her colleagues feared her accuracy. She faced some criticism for her pantsuit business attire, so she occasionally wore a businesslike skirt or slacks with a blouse. She wasn't concerned about appearing feminine; her only priority was being taken seriously.

Campaign rallies grew larger each week, more like a reality show than a political event. Paul thrived on spectacle, organizing photo opportunities at construction sites, veterans' breakfasts, and even an "unscheduled" visit to a small-town barbershop—cameras just happened to be there. He mastered social media, posting viral videos that mocked his opponents with the flair of a seasoned showman. The pundits said he was light on substance, but Paul knew better: in politics, stealing the spotlight was enough to count as substance. Speaking of stealing the spotlight, wife Maria was a big hit with the press and minority groups. Paul made sure to include her in his walks around town, to reflect more light on himself.

To be continued.

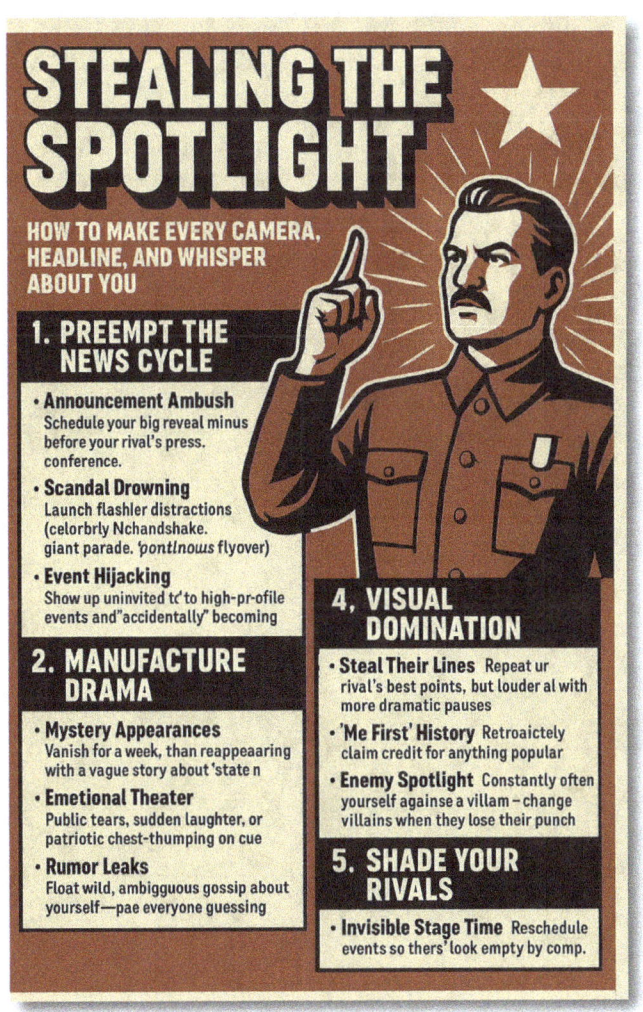

*Why follow rules when you can create your own? Control enforcers—judges, police, lawmakers—to amplify power.*

# Chapter 4

## Rewrite The Rules

*"Culture is why a nation can continue to inherit and develop. The essential primary carriers of cultural inheritance are very different. There are two types.*
*First, the written literature handed down from ancient times. The second is a physical type of literature.*
*It is architecture and construction, like the Great Wall."*

### The Art of Retroactive Legality
Rewrite history and the law—alter the official record so your actions are always considered legal. Backdate decrees— nothing shows "compliance" like signing yesterday's orders today. Create loopholes where none exist; lawyers will fill in the gaps and handle the paperwork afterward.

### Legal Shapeshifting
Flexible Interpretation – View the constitution as a dance that allows multiple interpretations. Overnight Amendments – Convene Congressional sessions at 3 a.m., ideally on a national holiday. Permanent "Temporary" Measures – Keep the sunset clause in place but never actually let the sunset happen.

### Control the Referees
Choose judges who are loyal and will follow your wishes as if they were sacred. Confirm puppet lawmakers – fill the

government with people whose only skill is enthusiastically nodding. Loyal "watchdogs" – replace regulatory agencies with symbolic mascots.

### Psychological Warfare Through Rules

Confuse the opposition by changing rules mid-game and claiming it was part of the plan. Use bureaucracy as a weapon by forcing rivals to fill out triplicate forms before every move. Overwhelm everyone with so many rules that they can't follow them all, then punish selectively.

### Bend the System

Constitutional Tweaks: Orbán rewrote Hungary's constitution in 2011, manipulating elections through gerrymandering (Journal of Democracy, 2019). Xi Jinping eliminated term limits in 2018, securing lifelong rule (NYTimes, "Xi's Power," 2018). Pinochet's 1980 Chilean constitution extended his rule until 1989 (Amnesty International, 2020). Museveni removed Uganda's term limits in 2005 (Human Rights Watch, 2024).

**Loyal Enforcers:** Bukele manipulated El Salvador's courts in 2021 to secure his 2024 re-election despite bans (NPR, 2024). Putin extended his presidency to 2036 through loyal judges (BBC, "Putin's Constitution," 2020). Pol Pot's 1975 Khmer Rouge tribunals executed "traitors" without trials (BBC, 2020).

**Decrees or Executive Orders:** Declare "Supreme Leader Day" or "mandatory applause," similar to Robert Mugabe's Zimbabwean law changes or Franco's post-war decrees banning dissent (BBC, "Franco's Spain," 2020). Prayut's 2014 coup decrees silenced Thailand's press (Amnesty International, 2020).

## Control the Gatekeepers

Bribery or threats: Offer "consulting fees" or reassign critics to what is called "Paperclip Audit." Erdoğan's 2016 purge of 100,000 judges and academics set a precedent (CRD, 2017). Suharto's cronyism from 1965 to 1998 rewarded loyalists with contracts (BBC, 2008).

**Parallel Systems:** Maduro's 2017 loyal legislature bypassed opposition, securing his 2024 "win" amid protests (New Yorker, 2024). Mobutu's 1970s "authenticité" councils marginalized rivals in Congo (BBC, 1997).

Example: Duterte's drug war empowered loyal police, bypassing courts, with over 20,000 extrajudicial killings (Human Rights Watch, 2022). Guelleh's 2021 Djibouti election used loyal courts to disqualify rivals (Africa Report, 2021).

**Pro Tip:** Suggest a "Patriotic Voting Act" that "accidentally" excludes opponents' voters. Gerrymander voting districts to give your party an advantage. Say it's "democracy protection." Study Pinochet's rigged referendums or Museveni's constitutional tweaks for ideas.

**Personal Development:** Modify family chore rules to benefit you. Appoint your dog as "Chief Enforcer." Practice by imitating Maduro's 2024 election rigging, Saied's 2021 parliament dissolution, or Pol Pot's kangaroo courts.

# An Ongoing Story

*Episode Four*

The city council's procedural handbook was thicker than any playbook Rob had ever seen—and far less fun. As Mayor, he became the head of the city council. But rules were flexible if you knew where to push. At a meeting, when an opponent tried to stall a vote, Rob smiled and said, "Well, the handbook does say we can move directly to a vote with unanimous consent. And I'm feeling unanimous." Laughter broke the tension, and the measure passed. Later, over coffee, a supporter told him, "You're a natural at this." Rob grinned. "Basketball taught me: if the rule doesn't work for you, change the rule—or the ref."

In her first board meeting as CFO, Margaret proposed a "strategic realignment" of the company's bylaws. "Just a few updates for efficiency," she explained smoothly—the changes centralized decision-making within a newly created executive committee—led by her. A skeptical board member raised an eyebrow. "Isn't this a bit... unconventional?" Margaret smiled. "Innovation often is." Two weeks later, the same board member was praising her "visionary restructuring" in a trade publication. Margaret had ensured that the board member secured a seat on the new executive committee.

The campaign team found out that the debate rules limited podium space to candidates polling above a certain level. This could mean Paul wouldn't qualify to share the stage with the other seven candidates. His solution? File a legal challenge against the polling threshold and hold his own "People's Debate" livestream. "Why let them set the rules," Paul told his strategist, "When I can set the stage?" The livestream drew more viewers than the official debate. On social media, Paul declared victory even before the moderators sat down.

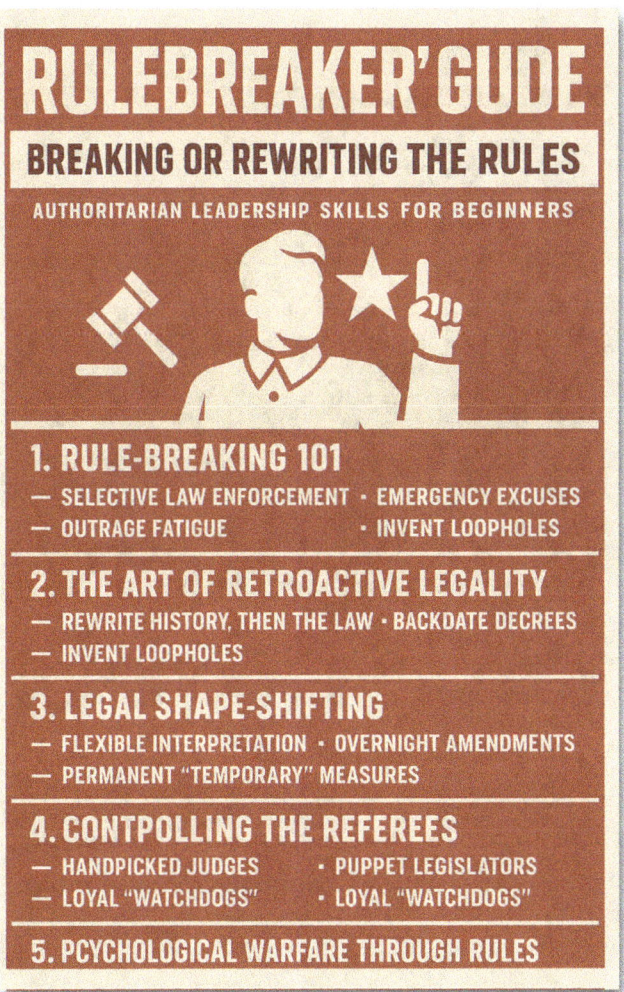

*"Only I can solve your problems and bring prosperity to your lives. On the first day I will create a million new jobs right here in your city. I will eliminate rush-hour traffic and electric cars."*

# Chapter 5

## Master the Art of the Political Speech

*A dictator's speech is like theater—think Mussolini's balcony rants, Castro's seven-hour epics, Putin's TV marathons, or a Trump rally. Captivate, confuse, facts optional.*

### Craft Your Delivery

Volume often takes precedence over substance. Leaders rally support with calls of "national destiny" or warnings of "enemies at the gates." Fidel Castro's lengthy speeches wore out dissenters, while Hitler's Reichstag speeches captivated crowds (BBC, "Nazi Propaganda," 2020). Use dramatic gestures—such as pointing upward or pounding the podium—to emphasize your points. Bukele's 2024 TikTok videos, featuring crown filters, depict a "cool dictator," hiding 70,000 arrests (NPR, 2024). By 2025, Putin's speeches blame "Western plots" for Russia's ruble crash, keeping supporters clapping (BBC, 2025)—a tactic that also fuels Daniel Ortega's anti-U.S. rants among Nicaraguans despite their economic struggles (Al Jazeera, 2021). Pol Pot's "Year Zero" speeches erased Cambodia's past (BBC, 2020).

**Pro Tip:** Complain about "traitors" causing slow Wi-Fi. If your cat runs away, you're not loud enough. Add a catchphrase: "We'll ban bad days!" Or "Glory awaits!" Study Suharto's quiet menace for contrast.

## Mastering Political Bullshit

According to Harry Frankfurt's book "On Bullshit_," this isn't exactly lying — it's a verbal fog of confidence and vagueness. Trump's 2024 healthcare dodge — "We'll have the best plan, tremendous" and echoes Mussolini's "trains on time" myths (NYTimes, 2024). Bolsonaro's 2025 X posts, claiming "rigged judges" block Brazil's "destiny," sidestep his coup trial (Euronews, 2025). Erdoğan's 2025 inflation denial — "globalist nonsense" — keeps supporters hyped despite 70% inflation (NYTimes, 2024). Mao's "Serve the People" slogans concealed the chaos of the Cultural Revolution (BBC, 2016). Museveni's 2021 "stability" speeches ignored jailed rivals (Human Rights Watch, 2024).

### Basic Bullshit Techniques *(see table 5.1 page 35)*

**Pivot:** On unemployment, say, "We're building a glorious future, jobs galore!" No stats needed.

**Deflect:** Blame "fake news" or "algorithms," like Maduro's 2024 "foreign conspiracy" claims or Lukashenko's "Western meddling" rants (BBC, 2020). **Distract** with bizarre social media posts typed all in caps.

**Repeat:** Flood X with #LeaderVibes: "Big wins soon, haters lose!"

**Pro Tip:** Answer "What's for lunch?" With, "A culinary revolution, the best meal!" If your family agrees, you're all set—Study Franco's monotone speeches or Prayut's military briefings for variety.

**Personal Development:** Mimic Trump's 2024 rally tangents by weaving grievances and word-salad BS into chaos. Livestream on X, accusing "shadow-bans" if views drop. Watch Bukele's TikTok clips, calling critics "jealous losers," Ortega's anti-imperialist marathons, or Pol Pot's genocidal rhetoric for delivery tips.

## An Ongoing Story

### Episode Five

The city festival was the first post-election speech for Rob. His notes were simple: three bullet points, none of them detailed. He started strong, saying, "Now that I'm Mayor, our city's best days aren't behind us—they're on the schedule for next season!" The crowd chuckled, unsure if it was a joke. "When will you get started with the modernization of the water filtration plant?" A reporter then asked about the specifics of his plan.

Rob smiled and said, "We have the best plan. Tremendous. You're going to love it." His supporters cheered as if he'd just shared a miracle.

The corporate earnings call was Margaret's stage, and she knew it. The numbers were just part of the performance. "We are entering a phase of transformative synergy," she told shareholders, pausing for effect. A junior analyst whispered to a colleague, "What does that mean?" The colleague shrugged. Margaret continued, sprinkling buzzwords—"innovation pipeline," "market recalibration," "strategic horizons"—without ever addressing the disappointing quarterly results. By the end, the stock price rose two points.

Rally speeches were partly unintentional stand-up comedy and partly an infomercial. Paul said, "Folks, they tell me we can't fix the economy. I say—we already have!" The crowd cheered. "They tell me the system's broken. I say—we'll rebuild it in gold!" A journalist tried to press him afterward on policy details. Paul leaned into the camera: "The only policy you need to know is that America wins, and losers don't get a say." His campaign store sold out of "Winners Only" caps the next day.

News reports revealed that during his third marriage, Paul had an affair with a colleague's wife. She disclosed the story to a third party after she was divorced and Paul married someone else. Paul told the press it was all a hoax created by his opponents, and that he didn't know who she was. "There are a lot of people out there who don't want this country to go back to strong moral values. So, they invent these "woke" conspiracies to make me look bad. Maria and I are happy together."

To be continued.

**TABLE 5.1**

# MASTERING THE ART OF POLITICAL BULLSHIT

| TECHNIQUE | HOW IT WORKS | EXAMPLE IN ACTION |
|---|---|---|
| DELIVERY | Style over substance— sound confident, even if saying nothing. | "As I've said many times before.... (never said it.) |
| DISTRACTION | Change the topic to samething more advantageous. | While we're talking about that, have you seen the stock market? |
| BLAME | Always have a target— never yourself, | "Clearly this is the opposition's mess, not ours. |
| MISINFORMATION | Supply a steady stream of "alternative facts." | Independent reports confirm.... (no reports exist) |
| VAGUE REPLIES | Speak in platitudes so broad no one can pin you down, | We are taking strong steps toward a better tomorrow. |
| LIES | Deny reality confidently and repeatedly. | "That never happend.' (It did.) |
| PIVOT | Redirect questions to safer ground. | That's a great question about policy—let's talk about jobs. |
| REPEAT | Say the same phrase until it feels true. | This is the greatest economy ever. Greatest ecomomy eves @txontor.nweez |
| WORD SALAD | Bury meaning in complexity and jargon. | Our multi-phase synergistic initiative |
| SCAPEGOAT | Assign all problems to one convenient villain | If not for linsert rival group, we'd be thriving |

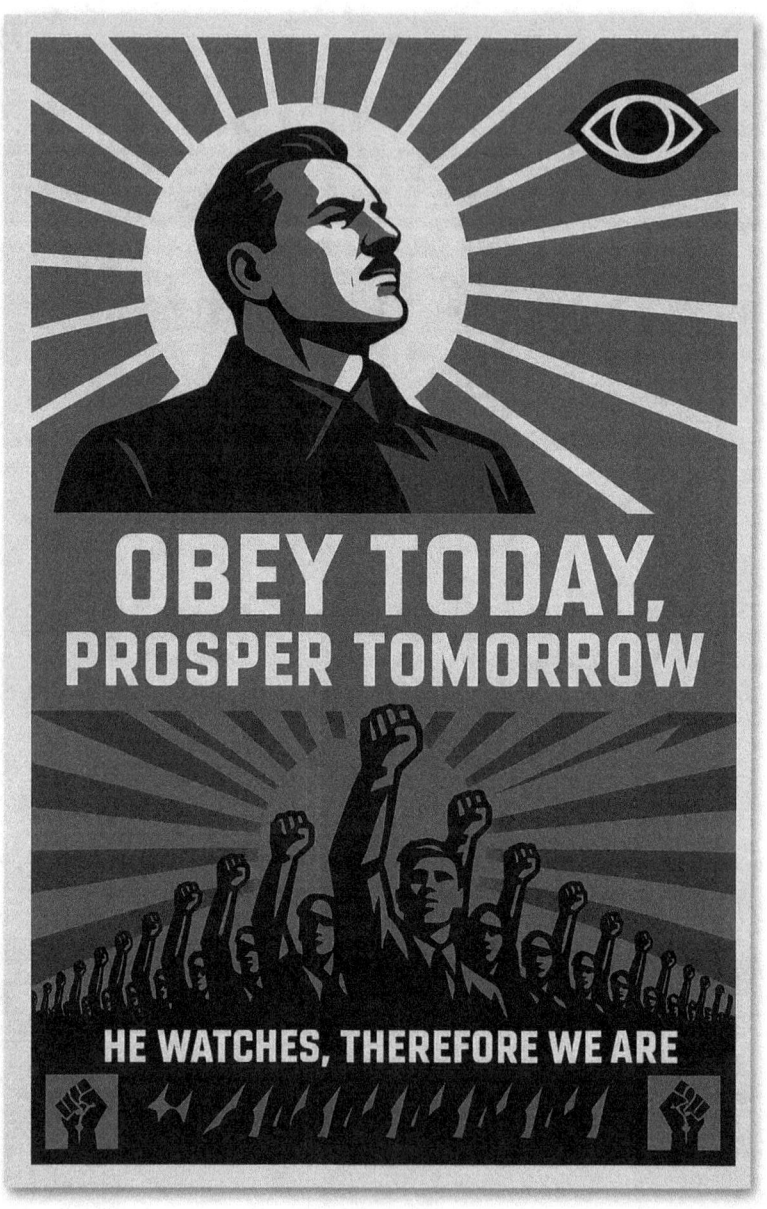

# Chapter 6

## Surround Yourself with Loyal Sycophants and Yes People

*No dictator governs alone. Build a team that cheers louder than a sitcom audience, prioritizing loyalty over intelligence. Recruit Sycophants who pass loyalty tests.*

An authoritarian leader needs staff who follow orders without question. They want people who will never make important decisions on their own—unilateral decision-making results in dismissal. The leader makes all the decisions on everything.

**Seek Adorers:** Find people who praise your every move, like Putin's siloviki, Trump's MAGA loyalists, or Mobutu's cronies in 1970s Congo (BBC, 1997). Reward them with titles such as "Chief Applauder." Guelleh's Djibouti cronies control port wealth (Africa Report, 2021).

**Punish Doubters**: Reassign critics to "Memo Sorting," echoing Mao's Cultural Revolution sidelining of intellectuals (BBC, 2016). Franco jailed or exiled dissenters after 1939 (BBC, 2020). Pol Pot executed "intellectuals" wearing glasses (BBC, 2020).

**Ignore Experts:** Chávez dismissed oil advisors, leading to Venezuela's industry decline by 2025 (Reuters, 2024). Erdoğan rejected economists warning of 70% inflation in 2025 (NYTimes, 2024). Suharto's 1998 crash disregarded financial experts (BBC, 2008).

*Spot Integrity (and Avoid It)*

**Red Flags:** People who say, "Have you considered the data?" or roll their eyes. Demote them to "Intern of Nothing."

**Loyalty Over Skill:** Appoint your cousin as defense minister, similar to Maduro's PDVSA cronies or Marcos's family appointments (Amnesty International, 2020). Blame "foreign sabotage" for failures. Choose incompetent people for executive roles.

**Example:** Trump's 2025 Pentagon pick, Pete Hegseth, a TV host with no governance experience, prioritizes loyalty (CNN, "Trump's Cabinet," 2025). Prayut's junta allies lacked expertise but secured Thailand's control from 2014 to 2020 (Amnesty International, 2020).

**Pro Tip:** Organize "loyalty auditions." Have aides write odes to your smile. If they hesitate, assign "Sock Drawer Duty." Study Amin's unpredictable promotions or Pol Pot's purges for chaotic energy.

**Personal Development:** Criticize Block X supporters, calling them "elite bots." Study Bolsonaro's 2025 trial, where loyalists like Eduardo Bolsonaro promote his "savior" story despite facing 40-year sentence risks (Euronews, 2025). Practice by mimicking Franco's loyalist purges or Guelleh's cronyism.

# *On Going Story*

### *Episode Six*

After winning the mayoral election, Rob quickly realized he didn't need the smartest advisers — he needed the loudest cheerleaders. He carefully selected a "community advisory team" consisting of his former assistant coach, his barber, and a retired neighbor who always nodded enthusiastically. When a policy meeting went off track, Rob leaned back and asked, "Do we all agree this is a good idea?" The unanimous chorus of "Absolutely, Rob!" was exactly the validation he sought. He appointed people he could trust to be loyal in key city roles despite their lack of experience. Any holdovers from the previous administration were tested for loyalty. Suspected apolitical or disloyal individuals were dismissed. Alleged failures of the previous administration were blamed on disloyal individuals.

As CFO, Margaret's first move was quietly removing anyone who challenged her strategy. In their place, she appointed a carefully selected group of loyalists—people who understood their role was to support her vision. During a tense budget meeting, a junior analyst hesitated over a proposed cut. Margaret faintly smiled and said, "I appreciate your perspective. Let's circle back after you've aligned with the rest of the team." By the next meeting, the analyst had transferred to a different department. The woman complained to the CEO about her transfer and accused Margaret of running a personality cult as CFO. After the CEO spoke with Margaret, the woman was dismissed without severance pay. Margaret told the CEO she was a troublemaker; she suspected her of leaking certain corporate correspondence to news outlets. This was an article she had leaked to her news producer husband.

The campaign team might not have been the most experienced, but their loyalty to Paul was unmatched. His communications director once called a major scandal "a genius move in disguise." Paul smiled proudly. During a strategy meeting, an aide suggested cutting the gold-plated campaign bus. Paul looked surprised. "Are you questioning the brand?" he asked. The aide quickly clarified, "No, sir. I actually think we should add more gold." Paul patted him on the back enthusiastically. "That's the spirit."

# SURROUND YOURSELF WITH LOYALISTS

## DICTATORSHIP 101

# FEAR TACTICS FOR ENSURING LOYAL SUPPORT

| TACTIC | HOW IT WORKS | EXAMPLE IMPLEMENTATION |
|---|---|---|
| RETRIBUTION | Remind everyone that betrayal is more expensive than loyalty. | 'Former aide now enjoys early retirement in a remote, undisclosed locat. |
| LOSS OF JOB | Tie careers to personal loyalty, not competence. | Sudden "performance review" after a suspected act of disloyalty |
| FAMILY PRESSURE | Exlend dissoyaiy.pg a public spectacle to deter others. | Cousin mysteriously reassigned to a less pleasant climate |
| PUBLIC HUMILIATION | Control assets; loyalty equals solvency | Televised "resignations" with scripted apologies |
| FINANCIAL RUIN | Show that loyalty is rewarded… for now | Bank account "maintenance fees" spike for suspected defectors |
| PARANOIA BY DESIGN | Keep everyone guessing about who's truly trusted | Loyalist of the month gets a new car; disloyalist of the month gets a bus ticket |
| THROW UNDER BUS | Blame and shame | Disgruntled ex-official blarned for recent policy failure |

*"If you tell a lie enough times, people will start to believe it is true." The Nazi minister of propaganda, Joseph Goebbels, is famously associated with the idea of repeating falsehoods until they are believed. While he may not have used this exact wording, the sentiment aligns with his propaganda methods. Authoritarian dictators are skilled at using this technique.*

# Chapter 7

## Create and Control the Narrative

Information is your weapon. Shape it like Goebbels' propaganda, Xi's Great Firewall, or Stalin's rewritten history, but without the dystopian tone.

### The Media and the Message

Freedom of the press in a democracy, along with Freedom of Speech, challenges authoritarian control. However, an authoritarian leader can also seize control of various media outlets and spread propaganda while claiming to protect free speech. By disseminating misinformation and labeling objective news as "fake," doubt is planted. Soon, it becomes impossible to distinguish between real and fake news. The propaganda is accepted as fact rather than challenged. The authoritarian promotes an alternative reality by spreading lies.

'In today's world, social media platforms like Twitter (now X) and Facebook have a global reach. Under the guise of free speech, they argue that they must allow all kinds of opinions. This creates an environment where authoritarians and far-right groups can spread misinformation, lies, and trolls to oppose democratic viewpoints. It's worth considering whether dictators control right-wing media and institutions or if those entities create leaders to match their ideology.

**Own The Story**

**Media Control:** Orbán is expected to dominate 90% of Hungary's press by 2025 (NPR, 2022). Other authoritarian regimes criticize the press as "enemies of the people' to intimidate them. In 2024, Maduro banned independent media, forcing outlets underground (New Yorker, 2024). Pinochet's media censorship in the 1970s silenced Chile's press (Amnesty International, 2020). Museveni's 2021 media raids in Uganda targeted critics (Human Rights Watch, 2024).

**Fake news**

Call truth "lies," like Trump's "alternative facts," Putin's "CIA plots," or Lukashenko's "Western meddling" (BBC, 2020). Stalin erased rivals from photos (BBC, "Stalin's Legacy," 2020). Pol Pot's radio claimed "utopia" amid genocide (BBC, 2020). These tactics must be used consistently by anyone trying to gain control of the government. In many countries, television is completely state-controlled and can be easily exploited for propaganda. An authoritarian leader can use bribery and intimidation to control privately owned media. Some privately owned outlets, like Fox News in the United States, support right-wing causes and broadcast propaganda as part of their sanctioned efforts programming.

**Rewrite History**

Claim you invented Wi-Fi, similar to Chávez's "revolutionary heritage" myths or Atatürk's erasure of Ottoman traditions for a "modern" Turkey (BBC, 2020). Suharto's "New Order" removed evidence of the 1965 massacre (BBC, 2008).

## Use Technology

### Bots and Deepfakes

Bolsonaro's 2023 WhatsApp forwards fueled riots (Euronews, 2023). Bukele's 2024 TikTok videos drown out critics of his arrests (NPR, 2024). TikTok has an international audience. Assad's 2025 state media spins war victories despite losses (UN, 2024). Prayut's administration from 2014 to 2020 in Thailand silenced dissent (Amnesty International, 2020).

### Censor Critics

Label journalists as "enemies of the people," as Trump did, or ban them, like Maduro's 2024 crackdowns. Duterte's harassment silenced Rappler's Maria Ressa (Human Rights Watch, 2022). Guelleh's 2021 Djibouti internet shutdowns blocked protests (Africa Report, 2021).

**Pro Tip:** Build a "Ministry of Truth" by sharing AI videos of yourself rescuing kittens. Blame scandals on "globalist algorithms." Study Goebbels' radio scripts, Stalin's photo purges, or Pol Pot's radio propaganda to learn about managing narratives.

**Personal Development:** Post social media rants about "winning big." Mimic Orbán's 2025 media empire, drowning out EU critics with #HungaryFirst hashtags, Marcos's 1970s propaganda films, or Museveni's radio control.

# An Ongoing Story

### Episode Seven

It didn't take long for Rob to realize that shaping the story mattered more than being truthful. When a local paper challenged his budget figures, Rob went live on social media and TikTok from a road repair site. "Look at these hardworking crews!" he said, with the camera focusing on workers who weren't fixing his district. The next day's headlines weren't about budget math—they were about Rob "getting results."

He started thinking about his next move, whether to run for governor or for a Senate seat. Gaining national recognition was crucial. Rob needed to craft a story that would qualify him for higher office. He read about Margaret Miller and decided to contact her about building a new manufacturing plant in the town. After the meeting, he announced that he had met with a top executive at her company and was negotiating with national and international firms to bring new jobs to the city. He also secured a Wall Street Journal article about his town and his efforts to increase job opportunities. Rob achieved the national exposure he was aiming for.

Understanding corporate storytelling better than most authors was Margaret's specialty. When quarterly losses loomed, she launched a glossy internal newsletter titled The Road Ahead, filled with stories of "record-breaking innovation" and "historic opportunities." She highlighted her outreach to rural American towns and efforts to build a manufacturing base, specifically mentioning her meeting with Mayor Rob Stevenson. A board member raised a concern during a meeting, and Margaret responded smoothly, "I think the data speaks for itself. And it's speaking very optimistically." The board nodded in agreement, feeling uncertain about the numbers but confident in the message.

Drowning out criticism with distractions and chaos is something Paul S. Johnson knew how to do. When a damaging investigative report aired, Paul immediately announced a "special broadcast" that night, unveiling a new campaign jingle, a large flag backdrop, and a surprise celebrity endorsement. At the rally, he criticized foreign countries for unfair trade policies. He promised to address the issue when he became president. The next day, the media barely mentioned the report. They focused on the unfair trade practices of Europe and China, according to P. S. Johnson. "Bad news only sticks," he told his team, "If you leave the wall empty. We cover it with BS."

*"When I'm elected the airlines WILL run on time"*

# RIVAL TACTICS COMPARISON CHART

## DEALING WITH AND ELIMINATING RIVALS

| TACTIC | HOW IT WORKS | PROS | CONS |
|---|---|---|---|
| Co-Option | Give rivals grand titles, meaningless jobs, and ceremonial ribbons to cut. | • Neuters their ambition.<br>• Makes you look 'inclusive'.<br>• Keeps them too busy for coups. | • They might gain influence.<br>• Can still plot in the shadows.<br>• Public asks, 'What do they do?' |
| Divide & Conquer | Stoke rivalries, spread rumors, and let factions fight each other. | • No bloodshed.<br>• Looks diplomatic.<br>• Rivals may enjoy their exile | • They might turn exile into a power base<br>• Memory of your flaws fades |
| Sidelining | Send rivals to distant posts, fake committees, or remote ambassadorships. | • They might turn exile into a power base.<br>• Memory of your flaws fades | • Loses skilled operators.<br>• Creates martyrs<br>• Power vacuum invites worse threats |
| Purge | Eliminate rivals completely in one decisive sweep. | • Removes all immediate threats.<br>• Creates a fearful. obedient inner circle | • Loses skilled operators.<br>• Creates martyrs<br>• Power vacuum invites worse threats |

# Chapter 8

## Dealing with and Eliminating Competition

*Publicly attacking rivals, both current and former, reveals weakness.*

**Golden Rule of Rivalry Management**

*A dictator should be like a gardener: prune carefully, let the weeds fight among themselves, and never burn down the entire garden unless you are willing to live in the ashes.*

Rivals are obstacles. Handle them quietly, avoiding Putin's "permanent sabbaticals," Stalin's purges, Pol Pot's killing fields, or Trump's Retribution. (These tend to attract unwanted media attention and—worse—Netflix documentaries.)

Authoritarian survival is a fragile game of chess played with people who don't realize they're on the board... until they're suddenly removed. In countries where dictators rise through democratic channels, rivals can multiply quickly—especially those annoying former allies who understand they helped build the throne you're sitting on. How you handle them decides whether you hold power for decades... or deliver a tearful farewell speech on live TV.

Another poor decision is pursuing retribution or revenge against individuals for perceived slights or imagined past transgressions. This may discourage some people from disloyalty, but it creates a negative image with the public—one of a petty, incompetent tyrant with nothing better to do. Going after government agencies that are simply doing their job in opposing some of your decisions previously or currently, damages the public in the long run. Without public support and acceptance, a dictator's days are numbered. Putting incompetent loyalists in charge of critical infrastructure shows disregard for voters and supporters.

## The CO-Option Technique

The saying "keep your friends close and your enemies closer" means it's smart to stay close to your friends while also closely watching your enemies. This helps you understand their actions and motives, potentially stopping their plans or exploiting their weaknesses. It emphasizes the importance of knowing both your allies and your enemies.

**Pros:** Turns ambitious enemies into overpaid furniture.
Keeps dangerous individuals too busy attending meetings to plot against you.
Helps you appear "inclusive" to the gullible public

**Cons:** The risk is that they might enjoy the fake job so much that they gain real influence.
Sooner or later, someone will ask, "What exactly does the Deputy Director of National Unity do?"

Assign minor roles to opponents, unlike Stalin's deadly purges of Trotsky or Bukharin (BBC, 2020). Pinochet co-opted moderate socialists to weaken opposition (Amnesty International, 2020). Suharto bribed military rivals (BBC, 2008). Divide: Pit aides against each other to foster rivalry rather than rebellion, like Mao's Cultural Revolution infighting (BBC, 2016). Pol Divide and Conquer. Encourage rival factions to dislike each other more than they dislike you. Spread gossip, share rumors, and occasionally "accidentally" leak the wrong memo to the right person. Pay special attention to certain individuals to make their coworkers resent them.

**Pros:** Keeps rivals too busy backstabbing each other to stab you. You become the "calm, steady leader" in a sea of chaos you created. Excellent entertainment value.

**Cons**: Requires ongoing maintenance—like feeding tropical fish, but with more venom. If they realize you're the common enemy, congratulations: you've just unified your opposition.

### The Sidelining Strategy

This strategy involves transferring non-political bureaucrats, such as those working in Health and Human Services or Veterans Affairs, to roles where they have no authority to act, since their replacements are political appointees. They will continue their work, but only the department head will see their actions and recommendations. Offer them severance pay if they choose to resign.

### Sideline Threats Quietly

Reassign: Shift competitors to "Form Filing," similar to Erdoğan's 2016 academic purges (CRD, 2017). Franco exiled Spain's intellectuals after 1939 (BBC, 2020). Museveni imprisoned Bobi Wine in 2021 (Human Rights Watch, 2024). Smear: Spread rumors that they dislike pizza, like Bolsonaro's 2025 judge attacks (Euronews, 2025). Mobutu called opponents "Western puppets" in the 1970s (BBC, 1997). Prayut accused Thai activists of being "communists" (Amnesty International, 2020). Banish: In 2024, Maduro banned opposition leaders, including María Corina Machado, sparking protests (New Yorker, 2024). Duterte's legal harassment crushed Philippine critics (Human Rights Watch, 2022). Guelleh disqualified Djibouti rivals in 2021 (Africa Report, 2021).

**Purges**: Removing all threats in a single bold move may be tempting. The dictator's dream: a fresh start with a cabinet of loyalists who tremble. This approach can lead to chaos and negative publicity, especially when a free press is still present. It also leaves no one in the shadows to control the situation. Purges of top military leaders often lead to low morale among officers and soldiers. In some countries, it could even trigger a military coup.

**Purges May Backfire**
While an authoritarian might succeed in removing rivals or competitors from their ranks, they can also eliminate the most intelligent and experienced individuals around them. What remains are sycophants and those who are afraid to offer an honest opinion. Purging the military of officers with high education levels weakens the decision-making process during conflicts. A wise leader avoids purges driven by revenge or false accusations of disloyalty.

**The Loyalty Gap:** Replacing ambitious rivals with terrified sycophants, and suddenly no one warns you when your "brilliant plan" turns into a disaster.

**The Skill Drain:** You just fired the people who knew how to manage the government. Incompetencies rises.

**The Power Vacuum:**
Removing rivals opens room for new, unknown threats—often worse than the ones before. Creating martyrs unites the opposition in direct proportion to your tendency to eliminate political opponents.

**Pro Tip:** Create a #RivalsLose hashtag. Challenge coworkers to a "loyalty stare-down." Study Amin's unpredictable rival purges, Pol Pot's executions, or Museveni's arrests for chaotic inspiration.

**Personal Development:** Mimic Saied's 2021 parliament dissolution in Tunisia, sidelining rivals with "emergency" decrees (Al Jazeera, 2022). Spread X rumors about opponents' poor music taste or imitate Marcos's 1972 opponent arrests or Prayut's activist crackdowns.

# An Ongoing Story

*Episode Eight*

Until a state representative began criticizing his budget priorities, Rob's rise on the local, state, and national scene had been smooth. He talked with friends on the state budget appropriations committee and managed to get the critic removed from the committee. Then, he issued a press release praising the critic's "new role" as chair of the "Special

Committee for Municipal Archival Records." It's an obscure position that involves organizing decades-old paperwork. "I'm recognizing his talents where they can shine," Rob told reporters with a straight face. The critic was not heard from afterward.

Climbing the corporate ladder is not without challenges. A vice president began questioning Margaret's aggressive restructuring. Within a month, the VP was "promoted" to lead an overseas division—complete with a nice office in a market the company planned to leave. Over champagne, another executive said, "You handled that... elegantly." Margaret smiled. "Sometimes you just need to give people space to grow."

Primary rivals were increasing—and so were the attack ads. Paul's strategy? Drown them in ridicule. "Candidate Smith," Paul declared at a rally, "is a fine man—if you're seeking a tour guide at a history museum." The crowd laughed, and the clip went viral. Another opponent dropped out after Paul's team leaked an embarrassing old video. "Politics isn't personal," Paul told his campaign manager, "it's just better when it's entertaining." He gave his rivals derogatory nicknames, such as calling one shorter man "Little Johnnie."

*In authoritarian horticulture, dissent is a weed, and ambition is an invasive species. Regular pruning ensures only the most obedient blossoms remain in bloom. Replace wilting officials with fresh, compliant buds, and always keep the compost heap ready — it's remarkable how quickly yesterday's allies can fertilize tomorrow's loyalty.*

*Pruning the Garden of Past and Present Unwanted Blooms.*

# DICTATOR'S GARDENING TIPS

*\*From the desk of the Ministry of Horticultural Harmony*

1. **PRUNE EARLY, PRUNE OFTEN**
   Rival branches grow fastest in spring — cut them before they flower into opposition.

2. **FERTILIZE WITH FEAR**
   A healthy dose of intimidation keeps roots obedient.

3. **ROTATE YOUR CROPS**
   Swap out old loyalists before they start dreaming of planting their own gardens.

4. **CONTROL THE SUNSHINE**
   Only let the approved blossoms bask in the spotlight; keep others in the shade.

5. **COMPOST THE DISCARDED**
   Yesterday's allies make excellent mulch for today's regime.

6. **BEWARE OF HIDDEN SEEDS**
   Dissent can sprout anywhere — even in your prized rose bushes.

*The Motherland Calls* is a massive statue in Volgograd, Russia, honoring the Soviet victory at the Battle of Stalingrad (1942–1943) during World War II. Designed by sculptor Yevgeny Vuchetich and engineer Nikolai Nikitin, it was finished in 1967. Standing 85 meters (279 feet) from base to tip of the sword, it was the tallest statue in the world at that time, symbolizing the Soviet Communist motherland calling her people to defend the nation.

# Chapter 9

## Build Monuments to Yourself

*Nothing screams "legacy" like your face on a billboard, a mountain, or a massive statue.*

*Preserve your legacy with grand symbols of your reign.*

There's no shortage of lavish monuments built by authoritarian leaders. They go all out to demonstrate who's in control. These striking structures are typically erected in countries ruled by autocratic leaders and right-wing regimes. The practical uses of these monuments are limited. They are meant to symbolize the greatness of the people who create them.

**Historical Examples**

**Arch of Triumph, Pyongyang, North Korea** – Built under Kim Il-sung, it's even taller than Paris's Arc de Triomphe. Massive, cold stone, military reliefs. It's deliberately taller than Paris's Arc de Triomphe and decorated with socialist realist reliefs and inscriptions.

**Palace of the Parliament, Bucharest, Romania** – Nicolae Ceaușescu's enormous government building, one of the largest in the world.

**Nazi Party Rally Grounds, Nuremberg, Germany** – Albert Speer's monumental stonework for Hitler's rallies, designed to awe and intimidate.

**Mausoleum of Mao Zedong**, Beijing, China – A grand, austere tomb in Tiananmen Square, flanked by statues celebrating "the people" (and Mao).

**Turkmenbashi's Neutrality Arch**, Ashgabat, Turkmenistan – A large tripod with a rotating golden statue of Saparmurat Niyazov on top.

**Victory Monument, Bangkok**, Thailand – Built by the military government in the 1940s as a symbol of nationalism.

**Heroes' Acre, Windhoek, Namibia** – Inspired by North Korean monument designs, featuring huge bronze statues.

**Gaddafi's Monument to the Resistance**, Tripoli, Libya – A giant fist crushing a U.S. fighter jet, serving as very literal propaganda.

If you're into statues, consider commissioning a bronze of yourself pointing heroically, similar to **Gurbanguly Berdimuhamedow's** golden effigies in Turkmenistan (BBC, "Golden Statues," 2015). **Saddam's** statues in Baghdad stood over Iraq until 2003 (BBC, 2003). Pol Pot's hidden memorials honored Khmer Rouge cadres (BBC, 2020).

Renaming buildings, historical sites, and streets after yourself is something supporters can do on your behalf. Rename a street to "Leader Lane,' emulate **Maduro's Chávez** murals in 2025 (New Yorker, 2024). **Mobutu** renamed Congo "Zaire" and cities after himself (BBC, 1997). **Museveni's** Uganda named roads after his 1986 victory (Human Rights Watch, 2024).

Rename whatever is possible after yourself or your significant other. Donald Trump has a Republican Congressional representative proposing a bill to rename the John F. Kennedy Performing Arts Center after himself (2025). Another supportive Representative is proposing Trumps head be carved into Mount Rushmore.

It's all about branding and marketing yourself. Put your selfie on mugs, claiming "cultural heritage." Kim Il-sung's lapel badges or pins are mandatory in North Korea (BBC, 2012). **Suharto's** "New Order" logos defined Indonesia's 1970s (BBC, 2008).

**Historical and Modern Examples**

**Kim Il-sung** (North Korea): Eternal flame towers and daily anthems overshadow Trump's branded hats. His statues remain sacred, upheld by Kim Jong-un (BBC, 2012).

**Viktor Orbán** (Hungary): By 2025, his Budapest "pride" museums will promote Christian conservatism despite EU criticism (ECFR, 2023).

**Indira Gandhi** (India): Her "Indira is India" posters flooded Delhi during the 1975–1977 Emergency, rivaling **Mao**'s "Little Red Book" craze (BBC, 2020). **Francisco Franco** (Spain): His Valley of the Fallen, built with forced labor, symbolized his rule from 1939 to 1975, although Spain started dismantling it in 2023 (BBC, 2020). **Prayut Chan-o-cha** (Thailand): His 2014–2020 junta built "Thai values" monuments, reinforcing military rule (Amnesty International, 2020).

**Pro Tip:** Host a "Monument Mania" contest where residents create your likeness using recyclables. Share on X with #LegacyVibes. Look into **Mobutu's** leopard-themed palaces or **Pol Pot's** secret memorials for examples of extravagance.

**Personal Development:** Suggest a national anthem that represents your wisdom. Mimic **Chávez's** constant murals, energize **Maduro's** 2025 propaganda, **Franco's** commanding monuments, or **Museveni's** victory roads.

*Arch of Triumph, Pyongyang, North Korea – Built under Kim Il-sung, it's even taller than Paris's Arc de Triomphe. Massive, cold stone, military reliefs.*

# An Ongoing Story

*Episode Nine*

After garnering more support in the city council and state assembly, Rob suggested a new community park—featuring a basketball court named "Stevenson Court." When a reporter asked if naming it after himself might seem pretentious, Rob grinned. "It's not about me. It's about inspiring the next generation… who will happen to see my name every day." The motion passed unanimously after he promised a ribbon-cutting ceremony with free hot dogs.

During her first annual conference as CFO, Margaret announced a new headquarters in Rob Stevenson's city. She understood that physical symbols hold significance in business. The building featured a sleek, glass-enclosed lobby and a large sculpture called "The Visionary Path," subtly shaped like her own silhouette. "It's abstract," she told a reporter, with a perfectly measured smile. "Interpret it however you like."

His campaign bus was already a moving tribute—painted with Paul's face, his slogan, and a flag design that looked strangely like a personal coat of arms. At a rally, he announced plans for a "National Renewal Center" in his home state, featuring a large gold dome. "It's not about me," Paul assured the crowd, "it's about America. And maybe a little about me." He unexpectedly won the primary elections. In just a few months, he became the President of the United States—an unexpected victory. Still, his campaign struck a chord with grassroots voters whose frustrations and fears he skillfully exploited. He convinced them that only he could solve their problems as an authoritarian leader. He promised to protect them from the enemies he blamed for their issues.

*Paul S Johnson wins Presidential Race with authoritarian platform. Promises to be dictator on first day!*

# DICTATOR'S
## ADMINISTRATIVE & TECH PLAYBOOK

*Because control isn't just about troops — it's about forms, firewalls, and facial recognition.*

| TACTIC | HOW IT WORKS | INTENDED EFFECT | POSSIBLE BAGFIRE |
|---|---|---|---|
| Selective Law Enforcement | Arrest critics for laywalking ignore uilles conmitling. | Lose papewoke of | Citizens notice laws are optional. |
| Weaponized Bureaucracy | Lose paperwork. delay permits, or | Builds a frusted inner circle | Burrpucacry can accidentally sabotage |
| Loyalty Appaintments | Lose appontent by-Paper | Builds a trustt inner *ciicle* | International aid groupe start |
| Surveiliance-by-Paper | Keep thick, dustey files | Creates fear of "being on the list." | People realize the erisis is you. |
| Legal Flooding | Bury opponents in lawsalts. | Reeps opposition guessing ws. | Too much data — drawning the |
| Predictive Policing | Reeps-oppositon gliessing who's a wa- | Nips desscent ifor "thinking about rroul or" | Arresting some- for 'thinking about |
| Censorship Infrastructure | Censerkshicas, fatrure blocks A cl. | Controls the nar | People create offline rumor ne |
| Mass Digital Surveillance | Manitors cails, email s, bd- movements. | Reality erases them from public | A troll defects. livestreaming yo. |
| Mass Digital Surveillance | Arresting someone for "thinking about trouble' | )Arresting same for"neurival | A troll defect — and banus distaus. |
| Disinformat-ion Factories | Censorship infrastruc-ture | People invent offline rumor ne | Someone hack. the system a too |
| Trall farms shutt down | "Maintenancce issues" shatt down prnt." | Maslinizes loyalty without debate | Al decide you" is low engagem |
| Enfrastructi-ure | Control rehrs eholos oreas—terie. | Opposittion can't covrdinate | Kule angry — phone calls |
| "Mainfenance issues" shut | "Maintenance issues" shut down *problem areas.* | Oppsisition can't coordinate | Blackouts affect vur supporters 1 |
| Control of Tech Infrastructure | Backsauts affecting public life | Control teck | Cue angry phone cails |

64

# Chapter 10

## *Weaponize Government and Technology*

*Tech is your scepter. Use it manipulate, monitor, and mesmerize.*

A dictator can manipulate government administration both through administrative means and technology by turning routine bureaucratic tasks and digital tools into instruments of control, suppression, and self-preservation. Here's an overview of how they might do it—using both administrative and technology-based approaches.

### Administrative Weaponization
Implementation depends on existing government structures, policies, and institutions, but it manipulates them for authoritarian goals.

### Selective Law Enforcement
Use regulatory agencies to target political opponents or dissidents with audits, inspections, and fines. Apply laws inconsistently — ignore small infractions by loyalists; prosecute minor missteps by critics. Go after anyone in government agencies who may have been involved in legal actions against you before you gained executive power.

## Weaponized Bureaucracy ("Red Tape Warfare")

Delay permits, licenses, or benefits for supporters of political rivals. Fast-track approvals for allies. Accidentally lose paperwork for opposition groups.

## Control of Appointments and Promotions

Staff courts, police, and civil service with loyalists instead of qualified professionals. Promote based on loyalty tests rather than merit. Have these new staff purge their departments of all civil servants who are not in your party or who were hired by the opposition in previous governments. Say you're cutting staff for budget reasons.

## Surveillance-by-Paper

Keep detailed records of citizens' political affiliations, movements, and associations under the guise of "national security.' Use census and social service data to identify and target specific populations. If needed, issue an executive order to create a new census based on criteria you decide should be used.

## Legal Flooding

Overwhelm opponents with lawsuits, defamation claims, or administrative complaints to drain their resources and time. Appeal all lower court rulings against your orders and the government to the highest court. If the highest court rules against you, ignore it.

## Weaponized Welfare and Public Services

Withhold social benefits, housing, or healthcare from areas that vote "incorrectly." Tie eligibility to public loyalty displays such as pledges, rallies, or party membership. Threaten to end disaster relief for areas that vote against you. Recall funds allocated for public services for reevaluation.

## Emergency Powers as a Permanent State

Declare indefinite states of emergency to avoid standard legislative review. Claim widespread criminal activity in urban areas where opposition parties are strong. Use special government police or the military to confront protesters. Blame crime on vulnerable minority groups or immigrants and randomly detain suspects. Deport them to detention camps.

## Technology Weaponization

Modern tools — including surveillance, AI, and digital manipulation — are used to expand reach and precision.

## Mass Digital Surveillance

Monitor phone calls, messages, and internet activity through government-controlled ISPs. Utilize facial recognition technology in public spaces to monitor activists and journalists. Threatening vague references to terrorism, check the cell phones of travelers and pedestrians.

## Data Fusion & Predictive Policing

Merge government databases like tax, health, education, and police records into centralized profiles for each citizen. Use algorithms to predict and prevent "threats" (real or imagined).

## Censorship Infrastructure

Control or restrict internet access; block sites critical of the government. Troll social media and harass regime protesters. Spread misinformation and propaganda favorable to you everywhere. Use keyword-based filtering to eliminate dissent instantly.

## Disinformation and Deepfake Factories

Use bots and troll farms to flood social media with pro-regime stories. Create deepfakes to undermine opposition leaders. **Examples:** Bukele's TikTok videos of gang crackdowns avoid human rights critiques (NPR, 2024). Putin's 2025 AI-generated "victory" clips deceive Russians (BBC, 2025). Museveni's 2021 campaign used bots to boost "stability" (Human Rights Watch, 2024).

## Digital Blacklists

Ban people from using public transportation, traveling, or applying for jobs if they are flagged as "security risks." Connect restrictions to ID-linked digital payment systems.

## AI-Driven Propaganda

Microtarget political messages and emotional manipulation to specific groups using personal data. Tailor news feeds to reinforce regime loyalty and demonize opponents.

## Control Critical Tech Infrastructure

Nationalize or directly oversee telecommunications, energy grids, and cloud services — allowing "technical malfunctions" in opposition strongholds.

## Track Critics

China's social credit system, which monitors 1.4 billion citizens, and Bukele's 2024 arrest-tracking technology set the standard (NPR, 2024). Assad's 2025 surveillance kept an eye on rebels (UN, 2024). Guelleh's Djibouti port technology tracks dissenters (Africa Report, 2021).

## Bot armies

Bolsonaro's 2023 WhatsApp riots and Orbán's 2025 #HungaryFirst bots illustrate digital influence (Euronews, 2023). Lukashenko's 2020 election bots drowned out protests (BBC, 2020). Prayut's Thai bots silenced critics from 2014 to 2020 (Amnesty International, 2020).

## Historical Precedents

Goebbels' radio: Nazi propaganda shaped narratives in the 1930s, similar to Xi's Great Firewall today (BBC, 2020). Stalin's censored newspapers suppressed dissenters (BBC, 2020). Pol Pot's radio broadcasts propagated 'Year Zero" myths during the genocide (BBC, 2020).

## KGB Surveillance

Putin's 2025 "sovereign internet" blocks Western platforms, echoing Soviet wiretapping (BBC, 2025). Suharto's phone taps in the 1970s monitored Indonesia's elites (BBC, 2008).

**Marcos's TV control** His martial law in 1972 seized control of Philippine media and broadcast propaganda films (Amnesty International, 2020).

**Pro Tip:** Create a "DictatorPal" app to track daily loyalty pledges. Deduct points when users send "frown" emojis. Look at Pinochet's 1970s phone taps, Pol Pot's radio lies, or Guelleh's port surveillance for retro ideas.

**Personal Development:** Post videos with crown filters, blaming "hackers" for glitches. Imitate Saied's 2022 social media crackdowns in Tunisia (Al Jazeera, 2022), Marcos's TV propaganda, or Museveni's bot-driven campaigns.

## An Ongoing Story

*Episode Ten*

"Go digital," Rob's nephew suggested for the US Senate elections. Soon, the modest campaign was flooding local social media with ads showing him shaking hands, fixing potholes, and even heroically helping a duck cross the street. When a rival complained about misinformation, Rob shrugged. "It's not misinformation — it's creative emphasis." A week later, a suspiciously positive "citizen poll" trended online. He received favorable endorsements from political and business leaders, including CFO Margaret Miller and the president-elect. .

The corporation invested heavily in analytics, and Margaret saw more than just quarterly returns—she saw opportunity. By monitoring employee engagement software, she identified dissenters early before complaints reached HR. "We're not spying," she told her executive team, "we're optimizing loyalty." A discreet series of targeted "motivational" emails soon had everyone enthusiastically aligned. After he was elected,

President Paul S. Johnson reached out to Margaret, who had supported his campaign. "Mr. President, congratulations," she said as she answered the phone. "I've heard good things about you and appreciate your ability and loyalty. I want to talk to you about joining our administration," he said. "Well, I'm honored to be considered. I'm happy here, but I'll talk with you," she responded. She would weigh whether it was worth joining an administration where her job wasn't secure. Johnson had a reputation for firing people for the slightest infraction.

The new regime launched an app called PaulPower, promising exclusive behind-the-scenes content. It acted as a direct data pipeline, gathering voter preferences, donation history, and even location data for rally turnout. When a reporter asked if it was invasive, Paul laughed. "Invasive? It's immersive. People love being part of the movement. And the movement loves knowing where its supporters are."

President P.S. Johnson reached out to his right-wing supporters as a dictator. He told them they would need to make sacrifices, but that it would be good for the country. He was making many changes to replace nonpartisan civil servants with loyalists who used technology to monitor social media for disqualifying information about current civil servants. All civil servants were required to sign loyalty oaths to P.S. Johnson or face termination.

To be continued.

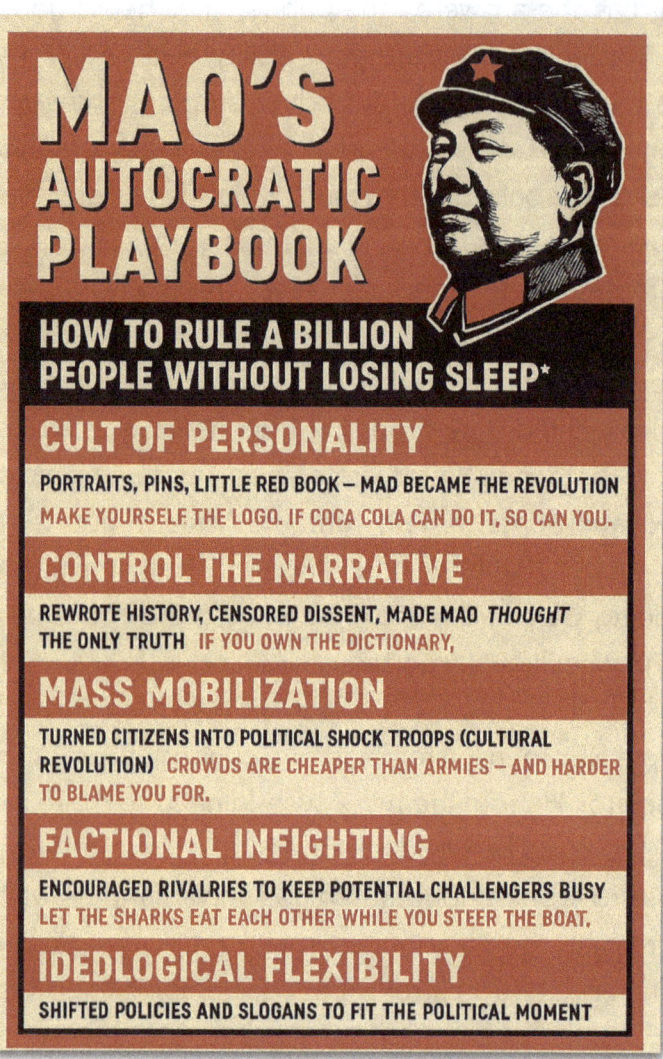

# Chapter 11

## The Autocratic Leader Playbook and Ignoring Advice

*Ignore all advice. You and your gut are the only experts. Trust your instincts. Ignore experts, historians, or reason.*

You and your gut are the only experts. Trust your instincts. Ignore experts, historians, or reason. Some authoritarian dictators may have started out consulting others before realizing it was a mistake. Trust your inner narcissist; you know it all. Everyone offering advice has their own agenda. You got where you are because you make the right decisions. Mao Zedong is a prime example of authoritarian decision-making. Recognize how many up and coming dictators today try to imitate his style of leadership.

**Mao Zedong's** policies, such as the Great Leap Forward and the Cultural Revolution, were implemented without significant public consultation or debate. They resulted in widespread suffering and loss of life. Mao Zedong can be classified as an authoritarian leader and dictator. He gained absolute power as the head of the Communist Party of China and the People's Republic of China for decades (1949–1976). He suppressed dissent and controlled all aspects of government and society. Mao's rule was characterized by the concentration of power in his hands. Dissent and opposition were not tolerated. Political opponents were purged, and the public was subjected to intense political indoctrination and propaganda. Mao built a strong *cult of personality* around himself, claiming his ideas were infallible and demanding unconditional loyalty.

Authoritarian dictators can learn a lot from Mao Zedong's long career in China. His portrait still hangs in millions of homes there. However, adopt his methods at your own risk. Mao's brand of authoritarianism does not work everywhere and didn't always succeed in China

### Distrust of Experts
Mao rejected technical experts and basic economic principles, favoring political solutions over technical ones during the Great Leap Forward. He sought to promote development through voluntarism and the organizational strength of socialism rather than relying on expertise.

### Emphasis on Self-Reliance
Mao emphasized China's independence in technology and industry, discouraging dependence on foreign technology, including that from the Soviet Union, especially during the heightened Sino-Soviet tensions.

### Centralization of Power
Mao consolidated power within the Communist Party and, later, through the Cultural Revolution, aimed to eliminate opposition and reestablish his authority, further limiting opportunities for dissenting voices and outside advice.

## Suppression of Dissent

The Hundred Flowers Campaign initially encouraged criticism, but it was soon followed by the Anti-Rightist Campaign, which suppressed intellectuals and anyone who criticized the Party and Mao's policies. This created an environment where challenging the dominant narrative was risky.

## The "Mass Line" Principle

While Mao promoted 'seeking advice from the people' as a principle of the 'mass line,' in reality, this often meant rallying the masses to carry out Party commands rather than genuinely seeking input on policy decisions.

Overall, the evidence suggests that while Mao may have, at times, listened to input during the earlier stages of the revolution and related to specific tactical situations, his general tendency, especially as his power became more consolidated, was to make decisions without significant input or challenges from experts or others, ultimately leading to policies with disastrous consequences like the Great Leap Forward.

## Trust Your Instincts
## Ignore Experts

Erdoğan dismissed economists in 2025, leading to 70% inflation (NYTimes, 2024). Chávez damaged Venezuela's oil sector by sidelining advisors, resulting in the 2025 collapse (Reuters, 2024). Mobutu's 1970s "Zairianization" ignored experts, causing Congo's economic collapse (BBC, 1997). Pol Pot's agrarian utopia overlooked scientists, leading to 1.7 million deaths (BBC, 2020).

**Deflect Failure**

Blame "disloyal aides," such as Putin's 2025-ruble crash explanations or Assad's "rebel sabotage" claims (BBC, 2025). Mao's Great Leap Forward failures were blamed on "counterrevolutionaries" (BBC, 2016).

**Example:** Mugabe ignored agricultural experts, which led to Zimbabwe's food crisis by 2000 (BBC, "Mugabe's Fall," 2017). Prayut ignored Thai economists, which hampered growth after the 2014 coup (Amnesty International, 2020).

**Adolf Hitler** ignored his generals' warnings, which resulted in the disaster at Stalingrad in 1943 (BBC, "Hitler's Mistakes," 2020). His instinct-driven invasions resemble Trump's 2025 tariff defiance (CNN, 2025).

**Ferdinand Marcos** sidelined economists during the 1970s martial law, accumulating debt and looting $10 billion (Amnesty International, 2020).

**Paul Kagame** (Rwanda): His leadership from 1994 to now dismisses critics of his media crackdowns, stressing "stability" over dissent (Human Rights Watch, 2024). His 99% election wins resemble Museveni's tactics.

**Suharto** (Indonesia): Ignored financial advisors in 1998, which helped lead to the collapse of Indonesia's economy during the Asian financial crisis (BBC, 2008).

**Pro Tip**

Your "gut reaction" is rooted in your emotional life experiences. It's not some mystical intuition from the universe. Instead, it depends on your personal interpretation of reality. Therefore, trust your gut reaction cautiously. It might just be your inner child throwing a tantrum or your narcissistic response to a situation.

**Personal Development**

Avoid books that challenge your narrative, such as Erdoğan's academic crackdowns, Marcos's library purges, or Pol Pot's destruction of Cambodia's libraries. Claim your policies fixed a "hidden crisis."

## An On Going Story

*Episode Eleven*

The campaign treasurer suggested they cut back on spending. Running for the Senate was more expensive than running for Mayor. Rob waved him off. "Voters don't remember balance sheets; they remember barbecues." When a volunteer worried about backlash over his pothole ads, Rob chuckled. "That's why we post more of them." The volunteer resigned two days later, and Rob replaced him with someone who agreed that the real problem was "negative energy."

With President P.S. Johnson's endorsement, Rob's campaign was able to raise more contributions. P.S. saw Stevenson as a future loyal supporter. Rob traveled across the state. "I fixed the potholes, I can fix the national government to help this state," he said. His campaign adopted the slogan, "Fix the Senate's Potholes, Elect Stevenson."

Margaret's board chair quietly advised her to slow down on restructuring. "Optics matter," he said. Margaret smiled thinly. "Optics are my specialty." A week later, the chair found himself sidelined from major decisions. When another executive warned her that her rapid changes were creating enemies, she replied, "If they're enemies, they were never on my side."

She entered negotiations with the P.S. Johnson regime for the Secretary of Education position, despite lacking previous experience in the field. She was also considered for the role of Secretary of Homeland Security. P.S.'s policy was to appoint loyal people to all roles in his administration. Their experience didn't matter because he made all final decisions. Margaret was not interested in subordinating her judgment and authority to anyone else.

Paul's S. Johnson's communications director urged him to tone down his rhetoric before the State of the Union Address. "It could alienate moderates," she said. Paul grinned. "Moderates don't buy tickets to the show." He planned to double down on bold promises and sharp insults. The director quit the next morning. Paul replaced her with a new spokesperson who opened her remarks by saying, "We don't apologize for winning." P. S. said she had nice lips and would do a great job.

P. S. Johnson relied on what he called "his gut reaction or intuition." "I'm never wrong when I trust myself and my gut decisions," he told his Chief of Staff. "I don't trust these experts; when I make decisions based on their opinions, I don't like the results." After his doubling down at the State of the Union address, the stock market plunged to a five-year low. "It's all a hoax, they are out to get me because I'm an outsider," P. S. ranted on his social media account.
To be continued.

**The Neutrality Monument** in Ashgabat, Turkmenistan, was built in 1998 during Saparmurat Niyazov's rule, the authoritarian leader better known as Turkmenbashi ("Father of all Turkmen").

Niyazov built a 75-meter structure to honor Turkmenistan's official stance of political neutrality, recognized by the UN in 1995. The monument's most notable feature was a 12-meter rotating golden statue of himself atop, designed to always face the sun.

The arch became a lasting symbol of Niyazov's personality cult, combining Soviet-style grandeur with a surreal, almost sci-fi look. It was taken down in 2010 by his successor, though the golden statue was relocated to another site in Ashgabat.

## DICTATORSHIP 101
### COMPARISON TABLE

| METRICS | 1 | 2 | 3 | 4 |
|---|---|---|---|---|
| Opportunities for Power | | | | |
| Image and Ego | | | | |
| Run for Office and Steal the Spotlight | | | | |
| Rewrite the Rules | | | | |
| Master the Art of Political Speech ad BS | | | | |
| Surround Yourself with Sycophants Proven Loyalists and Yes-People | | | | |
| Create and Control the Narrative | | | | |
| Dealing with and Eliminating Competition | | | | |
| Building Monuments to Oneself | | | | |
| Autocratic Government and Technology | | | | |
| Autocratic Leader | | | | |

*Mark each leader's achievements in the table. Use ✓ for "fully mastered," ▲ for "aspiring," and X for "needs remedial despot training." Creative substitutions are welcome. Bonus points for spectacular scandals.*

### SCORING KEY

**FULL MASTERY**
Textbook authoritarian excellence. Could teach a masterclass.

**ASPIRING**
Shows promise but may need a coup, scandal, or dramatic speech to level up.

**NEEDS WORK**
Still clinging to quaint democratic habits – unacceptable

**BONUS STAR**
Awarded for flair – the kind that gets monuments built and constitutions rewritten

# Chapter 12

## Authoritarians Who Have Made Their Marks

*"The people must be so disciplined they do not even dare to think."* — Pol Pot

Analyze these profiles of established authoritarian leaders—Putin, Xi, Orban—and an emerging wannabe dictator, Trump. This isn't an exhaustive list of dictators, but these individuals largely follow the principles, standards, and ideas discussed in *Dictatorship 101* for establishing an authoritarian regime. They have different histories and have come to power in different ways.

**Authoritarian Leaders**

**Vladimir Putin: Russia's Puppet Master**
Vladimir Putin is a Russian politician and former intelligence officer who currently serves as the President of Russia. He was born on October 7, 1952. He previously served as Prime Minister and has been in his current presidential role since 2012, after serving as President from 2000 to 2008. He also served as Prime Minister from 1999 to 2000 and again from 2008 to 2012. He is the longest-serving Russian or Soviet leader since Joseph Stalin. As President of Russia, it is reported that he has accumulated significant wealth. A former KGB officer turned president (1999–2008, 2012–present), Putin used the Chechen wars and the chaos of the 1990s under Yeltsin to rise

to power, demonstrating strength through shirtless photo ops (BBC, "Putin's Rise," 2020)

Putin enacted constitutional amendments extending until 2036, framing RT's "savior" narrative and engaging in rival "sabbaticals," such as Alexei Navalny's 2021 poisoning and imprisonment (BBC, 2021). In 2022,

Putin

he invaded Ukraine, a neighboring sovereign country. He suppresses dissent in Russia, and men are conscripted to fight in Ukraine. The invasion continues into 2025. His "sovereign internet" restricts dissent, similar to Xi's Great Firewall (BBC, 2025). His purges resemble Stalin's 1930s Great Terror, killing millions (BBC, 2020).

Loyal oligarchs, siloviki[1] and media control remain strong, even as sanctions take effect. His tactics resemble Suharto's military dominance (BBC, 2008).

## Xi Jinping, Chairman for Life, etc., China

Xi Jinping (born June 15, 1953) is a Chinese politician who has served as the general secretary of the Chinese Communist Party (CCP), chairman of the Central Military Commission

1       Siloviki (singular: silovik) in Russia refers to individuals with backgrounds in the military, security services, or law enforcement, according to DoctorParadox.net and Wikipedia. Specifically, the term includes those who have worked for or are currently working for the "ministries of force" (silovye ministerstva), which hold coercive power on behalf of the state. These "force structures" include, but are not limited to, the armed forces, police, security agencies such as the FSB and GRU (military intelligence), and other related organizations.

(CMC), and thus the top leader of China since 2012. Since 2013, Xi has also been the seventh president of China. As a member of the fifth generation of Chinese leadership, Xi is the first CCP general secretary born after the founding of the People's Republic of China (PRC).

Xi Jinping is regarded as one of the most successful members of the Princelings, a semi-clique of politicians who are descendants of early Chinese Communist revolutionaries. When asked about Xi, former Singaporean Prime Minister Lee Kuan Yew said he believed Xi was "a thoughtful man who has gone through many trials and tribulations."

*Xi Jinping*

Xi's history and rise to power occurred over decades within a system that is structured and grounded in Communist Party ideology. This system is authoritarian in nature, and its first leader was Mao Zedong.

Since taking power, Xi's leadership has seen a significant rise in censorship and mass surveillance, a decline in human rights (including the persecution of Uyghurs), the emergence of a cult of personality, and the removal of term limits for the presidency in 2018. Xi's political ideas and principles, known as Xi Jinping Thought, have been embedded in the party and national constitutions. He is a CCP cadre who has become "Chairman for Life." Xi has strengthened his authority through the "Chinese Dream" of global dominance (The New York Times, "Xi's Power," 2018).

Xi's early life was difficult during the Cultural Revolution, when his father was purged and he was sent to the countryside for "re-education" and manual labor. Despite these hardships, he joined the CCP and gradually moved up through the party ranks, holding various provincial leadership roles before reaching the highest levels of power.

Taking on leadership in 2013, Xi has led major initiatives, including a widespread anti-corruption campaign and the Belt and Road Initiative, a global infrastructure development strategy. He has also overseen a strengthening of China's economic and military influence on the world stage.

However, his leadership has also faced criticism over human rights issues, especially regarding the treatment of Uyghur Muslims in Xinjiang, and his administration has been marked by increased government surveillance and censorship. In 2018, the removal of presidential term limits allowed him the possibility of staying in power permanently.

Omnipresent portraits on public display and in the media. Great Firewall censorship, social credit surveillance tracking of 1.4 billion residents, and "anti-corruption" purges, such as Bo Xilai's 2012 ouster. As of 2025, ghost cities persist, but dissent is crushed (Reuters, 2025). His cult mirrors Mao's Red Book mania (BBC, 2016). AI-controlled systems surpass Putin's regime.

### Victor Orbán Prime Minister Hungary

Viktor Orbán, born on May 31, 1963, is a Hungarian lawyer and politician who has been serving as Hungary's Prime Minister since 2010, and previously from 1998 to 2002. He also leads the Fidesz political party, which he has headed since 2003, and earlier from 1993 to 2000. Orbán was re-elected in 2014, 2018, and 2022, making him the country's longest-serving prime minister.

Orbán

Orbán's political career began in the late 1980s with the founding of Fidesz, which initially supported liberal and democratic reforms. He gained prominence after the fall of communism, becoming a vocal critic of the socialist government. His first term as Prime Minister (1998-2002) focused on economic reforms and efforts to modernize Hungary.

Since returning to power in 2010, Orbán's government has been defined by what he calls "illiberal democracy," which stresses national sovereignty, traditional values, and economic independence. This has resulted in increased centralization of authority, reforms to the judiciary and media, and policies that have faced criticism from the European Union and human rights organizations. His methods are similar to those of an authoritarian leader who has weakened the country's democratic roots.

## Up and Coming Authoritarian Dictator

*The Golden Escalator Ride to Dictatorship*

Donald Trump's remarkable rise from reality TV star to

*Trump & Kim Jong -un*

two-term U.S. president (2016–2021, 2024–present) exemplifies a form of dictatorship with MAGA hats, social media chaos, and few checks by a Republican-controlled Congress and Senate. He has a supportive Supreme Court. In seven months of his second term, he has shown traits of an authoritarian leader. He took control of the Department of Justice (DOJ), the FBI, the DHS, the NSA, and the CIA. Appointed loyalists now run all these agencies. He uses his political influence try to control higher education, law firms, businesses, and government agencies, including the dismantling of Departments like Education and Science, as well as other vital infrastructure. Using a paramilitary group (ICE) and National Guard troops, he attacks municipal areas where opposition and minority groups reside.

Trump's biggest problem is that he is a narcissistic, seventy-nine-year-old man determined to retaliate against all the insults and slights he believes he has experienced. He wants revenge for being prosecuted for criminal behavior for which he was guilty. He aims to undo everything that Presidents Obama and Biden accomplished during their presidential administrations. He seeks to remove all the military generals who opposed his unconstitutional wishes and dismantle all government departments that would not help him hide the COVID-19 pandemic. He is fixated on winning a Nobel Prize because President Obama, someone he used racist tactics to oppose, won the prize. His motivation is revenge, retaliation, and financial gain. His behind-the-scenes billionaire, right-wing supporters are using him to create a totalitarian environment they ultimately control.

**Key Moves**

Trump has been a manipulator of people and a showman his whole life His MAGA cap and "billionaire savior" aura rival Bukele's TikTok style. His 2025 posts showcase large crowds, despite a low approval rating (NBC, "Trump Approval," 2025). His branded towers and extensive merchandise keep his name and slogans visible in the public eye. The 2015 escalator entrance, racist remarks, and "build the wall" promises echo Mussolini's myths. However, they have left a lasting impression on both his followers and detractors. Despite being 79 years old, having 34 felony convictions, and influencing 2024 memes that sway voters (The New York Times, "Trump's Comeback," 2024), his impact persists. His rallies resemble Perón's populist spectacles (BBC, 2020). In his second term, he has dominated all media daily with attention-grabbing appearances, signing executive orders, hiring and firing staff, posting insipid social media messages, enacting tax hikes, negotiating with foreign leaders over tariffs, and other appearances.

The 2025 purge of "disloyal" bureaucrats bears resemblance to Orbán's Fidesz. His 2022 "Terminate Constitution" post hinted at a "Patriotic Voting Act" (NBC, "Trump Constitution," 2022). His tactics mimic Suharto's cronyism (BBC, 2008). He has ignored constitutional laws and court orders and has unilaterally halted laws and bills passed by Congress. His secret police (ICE) disregard Habeas Corpus laws and arrest immigrants and citizens without warrants. He is using federal troops to impose martial law in Washington, D.C. and he is threatening to do the same in other cities if there are protests. Trump threatened to ban mail-in voting and the use of voting machines by executive order in the 2026 elections -The New York Times, August 2025.

Loyalists, such as a TV host appointed Secretary of Defense, resemble Mao's unqualified cronies (CNN, "Trump's Cabinet," 2025). Museveni's loyalist appointments follow a similar pattern (Human Rights Watch, 2024). He has emptied government agencies of nonpartisan civil servants. Those he replaces are required to swear an oath of loyalty to him. He has also purged the upper military ranks of career generals, women, and people of color who refuse to take a loyalty oath to him.

The Trump regime promotes a narrative endorsed and spread by its leader through speeches and social media. He has unilaterally cut funding for Public Television and NPR Radio, even though Congress allocates funds to these agencies. "Fake news" and X bot armies resemble Maduro's media bans. In 2025, FCC investigations targeted major outlets, including CNN (Reuters, "FCC Under Trump," 2025). Pol Pot's radio lies serve as a grim precedent (BBC, 2020). Trump has threatened, intimidated media and entertainment companies, and demanded they pay his government large sums of money

His threats to prosecute former rivals and political opponents such as Biden, Harris, and Obama in 2025 are similar to Duterte's harassment (NYTimes, 2024). His "lock her up" chants echo Pinochet's enemy purges (Amnesty International, 2020). However, during the first seven months of his second term, he has ordered his Department of Justice to pursue legal action against those he believes opposed him in the past. Hundreds of DOJ and FBI career staff members have been fired because they carried out prosecutions related to his previous crimes.

Trump-branded towers and 2025 "pride" projects, such as proposed MAGA museums, compete with Orbán's displays in Budapest (ECFR, 2023). Franco's Valley of the Fallen reflects a similar historical comparison (BBC, 2020). He has his supporters suggest that buildings and monuments be built or renamed with his name on them.

Advice on 2025 tariffs and climate denial, despite economists' warnings, shows the same reluctance to listen as Erdoğan's refusal to acknowledge inflation (NYTimes, 2024). Suharto's 1998 crash was also preceded by similar warnings (BBC, 2008). Economic indicators have declined over the past seven months. Trump dismisses or ignores any information that does not support his actions. He uses distraction to cover his tracks.

**Adverse Factors**

U.S. institutions—courts, Congress, voters—limit Trump's authoritarian power, unlike Xi's unchecked authority. His 2021 impeachment, the January 6th attempted coupe fallout, and ongoing investigations (such as those into Epstein) demonstrate democracy's resilience (CNN, "Trump Investigations," 2025). The call from his base to release information about Jeffrey Epstein and his failure to deliver on promises, like lowering grocery costs, has cost him support. His 37% approval rating and midterm losses may weaken his influence.

## Conclusion

Trump's style echoes Berlusconi's media-driven populism, Perón's personality cult, and Suharto's cronyism, but U.S. checks and balances limit, to some extent, Franco-like control. Trump's mindset appears to be rooted in a transactional, corrupt business model. He tries all the typical dictator moves, but uses the power gained foolishly and for bragging rights. International leaders like Putin know how to flatter and manipulate him. His advisors are yes men, talk show hosts and conspiracy trolls. In his second term, he has caused significant chaos in his efforts to consolidate power, maintain control of Congress through midterm elections, pursue right-wing policy goals, and position himself to run for a third term in 2028. But Trump survives because he is supported by billionaire oligarchs who control and back him to achieve their own far-right political and economic goals.

# *An Ongoing Story*

### *Episode Twelve*

The TV footage of certain politicians making spectacular appearances inspired Rob. "An entrance like that," he muttered, "makes a ribbon-cutting look like amateur hour." He drew ideas from these memories for his next event. Rob staged his own "grand arrival" at the state capitol steps, emerging from a Budget moving van draped in campaign banners. Speakers mounted on the roof of the truck blared "Eye of the Tiger." The paid crowd of supporters cheered and waved flags. Big moves require big entrances," he told reporters, as if quoting a political masterclass.

She seldom admired politicians, but Margaret valued strategy. At the time, after noticing P. S. Johnson's aggressive branding and constant media coverage, she told her PR director, "Our quarterly reports need the same energy." The next investor presentation featured cinematic music, dramatic lighting, and an opening line that could have come straight from a rally:

"This quarter, we're not just meeting expectations—we're rewriting them." She noticed Johnson constantly branding himself and attracting media attention during his campaign and afterward. He was in the news every day. Most of the coverage he generated only increased the chaos. He invited her to join him for an appearance, but she decided she didn't want to be part of the president's show.

"Escalator entrances are so tacky," thought Paul. "A gold escalator? Amateur hour," he told his campaign staff. "We're going bigger, rock star!" At his next rally, Paul arrived on stage via a slow-moving, spotlighted platform that rose from below, accompanied by thunderous music. When the music stopped, he spoke. "Only I can solve the problems of this country and bring it back to a golden age." Many pundits attributed this stunt to his winning the election. When asked if it was over the top, Paul grinned. "If they're talking about the entrance, they're not talking about my opponents. No such thing as bad PR."

To be continued.

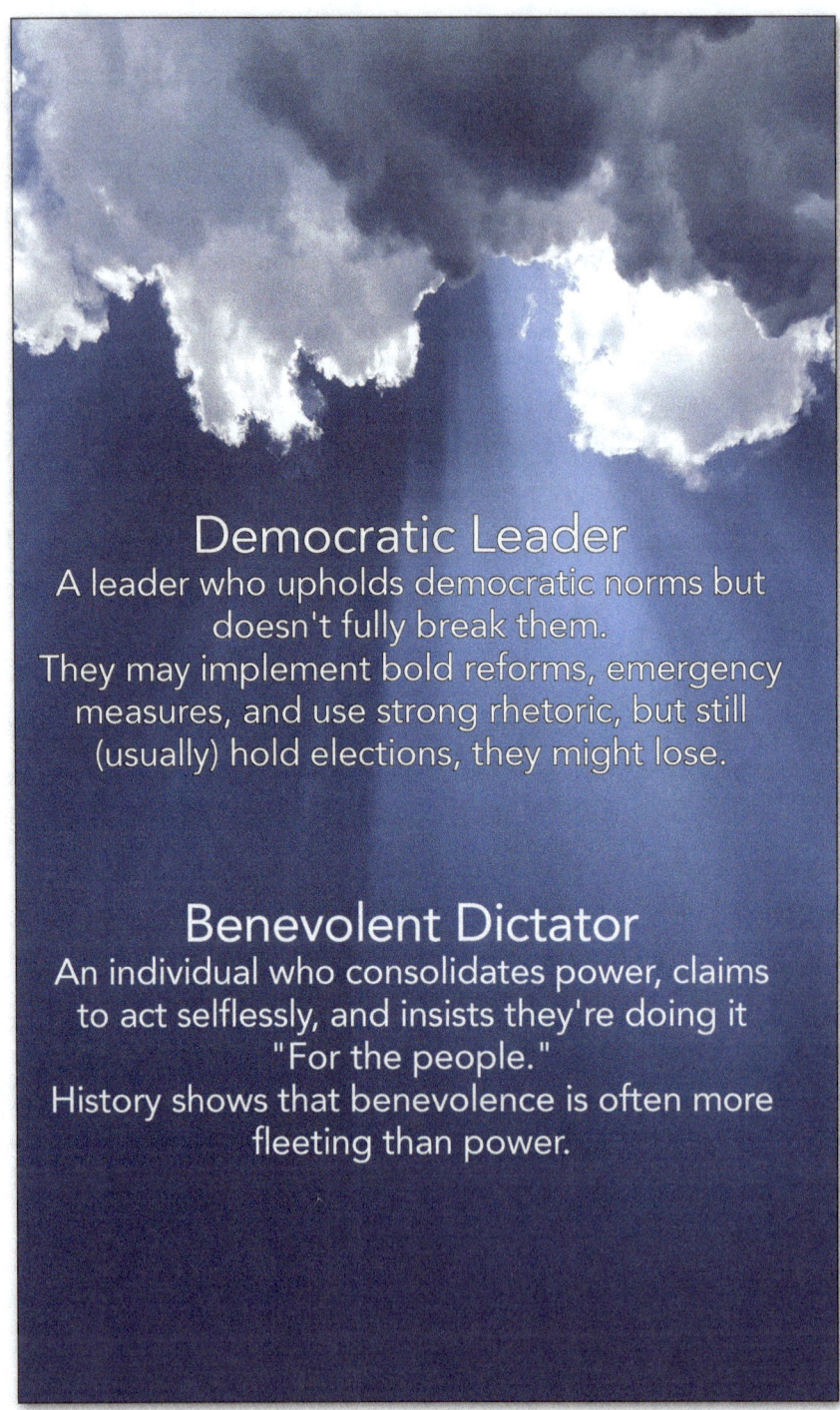

## Democratic Leader
A leader who upholds democratic norms but doesn't fully break them.
They may implement bold reforms, emergency measures, and use strong rhetoric, but still (usually) hold elections, they might lose.

## Benevolent Dictator
An individual who consolidates power, claims to act selflessly, and insists they're doing it "For the people."
History shows that benevolence is often more fleeting than power.

# Chapter 13

## *Benevolent Dictator or Strong Democratic Leader*

*The line between democracy and dictatorship isn't marked on the ground—it's sketched in pencil, and you're holding the eraser.*

## Benevolent Dictator or Merely a Strong Democratic Leader?

It's essential to understand how to distinguish between the mythical "benevolent dictator" and a true democratic leader with authoritarian tendencies. Spoiler alert: the line between them is blurry, subjective, and surprisingly easy to cross when power feels strong.

### *Checklist*

Behaviors from an elected leader who is leaning toward authoritarianism. They might be shifting from a "strong leader" to a "benevolent dictator."

✓ Expands executive powers "temporarily."
✓ Frames opposition as enemies of progress and the people.
✓ Governs by decree or executive order whenever possible.
✓ Declares, "The people want me to decide everything."
✓ Wins referenda with suspiciously high margins (90%).

Historically, several leaders have qualified as authoritarian-leaning democrats. Among the top three, there is one woman. It is worth noting that internationally, in government, few women rise to the authoritarian dictator level. Not many women become democratic or authoritarian leaders of their countries.

## Candidates for Authoritarian Democratic (Democracy) Consideration

**Franklin D. Roosevelt** greatly expanded presidential power during the Depression and World War II. His actions still operated within electoral and legal systems, although his court-packing scheme raised concerns, and he broke traditional norms by being reelected four times (1933-1945). He was widely liked and popular for his "fireside chats," broadcast on the radio. These speeches promoted New Deal reforms. A failed 1937 court-packing attempt tested limits, and dams like Hoover Dam became monuments to his presidency. His 1942 Japanese internment challenged democratic norms, including the internment of 120,000 Japanese Americans (NYTimes, "Internment," 2020).

Congress and elections restricted his power. The 22nd Amendment (1951) prohibits future presidents from serving more than two terms. Perón's Argentina provides a parallel (BBC, 2020).

**India's Iron Lady**

**Indira Gandhi**, Prime Minister (1966–1977, 1980–1984), daughter of Jawaharlal Nehru, promoted populist "Garibi Hatao" reforms (BBC, "Gandhi's Emergency," 2020). declared a State of Emergency (1975–77), suspended civil liberties, and jailed opponents. A "democratic" leader acting with authoritarian methods. Her 1975–1977 Emergency censored media, imprisoned 140,000 critics, and sterilized millions under population control. Ousted in 1977, she returned in 1980 but was assassinated in 1984 after Operation Blue Star.

Gandhi is remembered as one of the most powerful women in the world during her tenure. Her supporters cite her leadership during victories over geopolitical rivals China and Pakistan in the early 1980s, as well as her anti-poverty campaign, which earned her the nickname "Mother Indira" (a pun on "Mother India") among the country's poor and rural classes. Henry Kissinger described her as an "Iron Lady", a nickname that became associated with her authoritarian personality. Critics note her cult of personality and dictatorial rule of India during the Emergency. In 1999, she was named "Woman of the Millennium" in an online poll organized by the BBC. In 2020, she was named by Time magazine among the 100 women who defined the past century, alongside the magazine's previous choices for Man of the Year.

**Charles de Gaulle:** Architect of France's strong presidency. Accused of "personal rule," yet maintained electoral legitimacy. His presidency, from 1958 to 1969, centralized power during the Algerian War, using referendums to bypass parliament (History, "De Gaulle," 2020). His 1969 resignation after losing a referendum kept him democratic.

In 1962, de Gaulle rewrote the French constitution to allow for direct presidential elections, arguing it was "for the good of the Republic." It turned the presidency into his personal launchpad, bypassing the usual political machinery. Two years later, he doubled down with another referendum—because when in doubt, ask the people, preferably in a way that ensures they shout "Oui!"

De Gaulle understood that a messy parliament is like a noisy family dinner—everyone talks, nobody eats. His solution? Restructure the dining table so that only he had the fork. By appealing directly to "the people" through referenda, he bypassed legislators entirely. Of course, when your options on the ballot are "Yes" or "Yes, but louder," it's not hard to win.

### Other Examples

**Getúlio Vargas** (Brazil): His 1937–1945 Estado Novo coup combined labor reforms with censorship, echoing FDR but leaning toward autocracy. Ousted in 1945, he returned in 1951, dying by suicide in 1954 amid military pressure (BBC, "Vargas," 2020).

**Mustafa Kemal Atatürk** (Turkey): His rule from 1923 to 1938 was marked by one-party rule, which modernized Turkey by banning traditional dress and scripts, but also silenced dissent (BBC, 2020). Revered as a nation-builder, he inspired Erdoğan's nationalism.

**Prayut Chan-o-cha** (Thailand): His 2014–2020 junta rule promised "stability," but media bans and activist arrests made it more autocratic. Elections in 2019 restored civilian rule, but his influence persists (Amnesty International, 2020).

**Historical Parallels:** FDR's New Deal mirrors Vargas's labor policies, Gandhi's Emergency echoes Marcos's martial law, Atatürk's reforms resemble Paul Kagame's post-1994 Rwanda "stability," and Prayut's junta recalls Pinochet's Chile (Human Rights Watch, 2024).

**Pro Tip:** Reforms are beneficial, but avoid declaring a state of emergency—elections can be challenging—Study de Gaulle's referendums or Prayut's "stability" rhetoric for a look at democratic style.

## The "Benevolent Dictator": Fact or Myth?

The distinction between a Benevolent Dictator and a strong or autocratic democratic leader is one that political theorists, historians, and even democracy advocates struggle to understand. The idea often arises in business or tech circles ("If only one smart person could make all the decisions without politics slowing things down…"). It looks efficient, but history shows that benevolence is usually short-lived. Power without checks tends to lead to abuse—whether in FDR's court-packing attempt, Gandhi's Emergency Rule, or de Gaulle's extensive presidential powers.

# An Ongoing Story

*Episode 13*

While studying a news clip of Putin's bare-chested fishing trip, Rob made a "Note to self," he muttered, "image beats policy… again." His aide suggested a photo op fixing a park bench. "Too small," Rob said. Instead, he arranged to visit an urban neighborhood basketball court, where he joined the shirtless team in a pickup game. He stuck around long enough to get press coverage and to sink a basket.

In a meeting, Margaret leaned toward her COO and said, I read about how the leader of China eliminated term limits without much debate. We can do the same for performance reviews. Soon, a policy memo redefined "annual reviews" as "executive trust affirmations," permanently securing her leadership position with minimal paperwork.

"Kim Jong-un's military parades are campaign gold. Imagine that energy, but with better music," Paul told his event coordinator. "Choose a holiday and organize a military parade to celebrate my inauguration as President. We can name it Paul Stewart Johnson Day. I want the Secretary of Defense and the Cabinet to be in the stands. The marching soldiers should be saluting me."

There was significant controversy once word spread about the military parade. However, the president ignored it and moved forward with the event. It was poorly attended by the public, with the streets around the Capitol nearly empty. The tanks rolled by, accompanied by only a few spectators. A squadron of jets thundered over the Capitol, scaring the pigeons near the Washington Monument. Afterwards, drones spelled out his name in the sky above the Capitol. Rain washed the smoke away quickly. P.S. claimed on social media that millions of people lined the streets and that the parade was a huge success. When a journalist asked if it was excessive, Paul shouted, "Excessive? No, it's patriotic choreography."

## The Benevolent Corporate Dictator

In many ways, Chief Executive Officers (CEOs) are viewed as benevolent dictators. However, most CEOs are not exactly recognized for their benevolence. Corporate style authoritarianism from the boardroom might extend into politics. Tech giants like Apple, Amazon, Tesla/SpaceX and others have power comparable to that of nations, similar to the East India Company's colonial rule in the 1700s (BBC, "Corporate Power," 2024).

Maybe you dream of becoming a billionaire CEO oligarch—part of an international group of oligarchs linked to authoritarian leaders around the world. No more countries, just global conglomerates run by CEO dictators who answer to shareholders.

Shareholders, lawsuits, and regulators limit CEO power, unlike Putin's rule. Musk's 2025 X controversies and FTC investigations show such limits (CNN, "Musk's Battles," 2025). Public backlash, like the 2024 Amazon boycotts, reflects election losses for Gandhi or the pressures from Prayut's 2019 election (Amnesty International, 2020).

Nevertheless, a rising movement supports creating corporate-style governments in many regions worldwide.

**Pro Tip**: Run a startup, not a country. A bad Glassdoor review hurts less than #CancelCEO: Study Marcos's looted billions or Suharto's crony empire to learn about corporate greed.

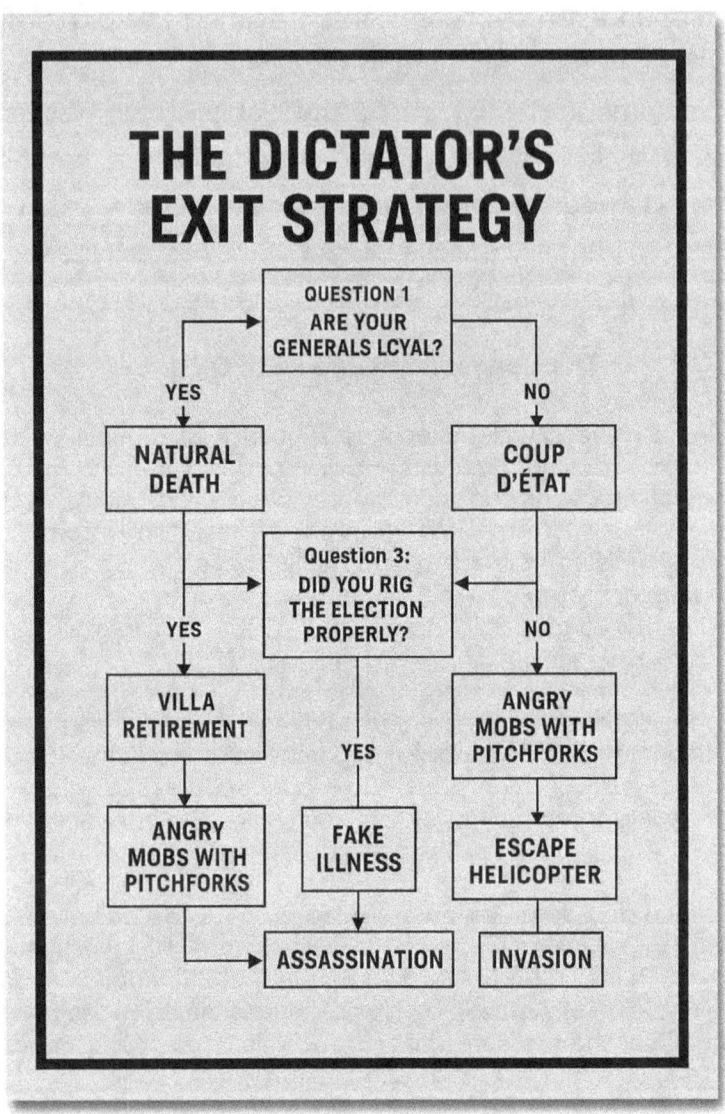

# THE DICTATOR'S EXIT STRATEGY

**QUESTION 1 ARE YOUR GENERALS LCYAL?**

YES → **NATURAL DEATH**

NO → **COUP D'ÉTAT**

**Question 3: DID YOU RIG THE ELECTION PROPERLY?**

YES → **VILLA RETIREMENT** → **ANGRY MOBS WITH PITCHFORKS** → **ASSASSINATION**

YES → **FAKE ILLNESS** → **ASSASSINATION**

NO → **ANGRY MOBS WITH PITCHFORKS** → **ESCAPE HELICOPTER** → **INVASION**

*The Authoritarian or Dictator's path is unpredictable. It's like a show on Netflix; it can be canceled at any moment, regardless of the polling numbers.*

# Chapter 14

## Exit Strategies for Authoritarian Leaders

*Because even the eternal dear leader must eventually pack his bags.*

*Power fades—sometimes gradually, sometimes suddenly. History shows autocrats fall through coups, revolutions, elections, or death. Here's how to avoid their fate (or at least plan a stylish exit).*

Every dictator believes he's invincible — or at least indispensable. Don't make that mistake. History shows that regimes, like fallen fruit, eventually rot. This chapter explores the two main types of authoritarian departures: *Traditional Exits*, sudden, messy, and often televised, and *Graceful Exits*, rare, usually negotiated, and always self-serving. Once you understand the variations, you can consider your retirement plan, should you survive that long. Consider starting a 401 (k) plan or an equivalent.

### A Brief Collection of Traditional Exits

Short List: Idi Amin was ousted by Tanzanian forces in 1979 after his unpredictable rule led to his allies abandoning him (BBC, "Amin's Reign," 2003). Mobutu fled the Congo in 1997 as rebels advanced and died in exile (BBC, 1997). Suharto resigned amid protests and military pressure in 1998 (BBC, 2008). Ferdinand Marcos's 1986 People Power Revolution in the Philippines forced him into exile in Hawaii, ending his $10 billion looting spree (Amnesty International, 2020). Nicolae Ceaușescu's 1989 Romanian uprising led to his execution (BBC, "Ceaușescu's Fall," 2020).

**Types and Causes**

These types of exits for authoritarians are not necessarily mutually exclusive. Non-dictatorial leaders can also experience these outcomes. However, dictators usually do not retire voluntarily. Authoritarians might be elected democratically but choose to stay in power indefinitely. Dictators may face coup attempts aimed at removing them. Still, most coups seem to be carried out by authoritarians trying to overturn an election they lost, overthrow a legitimately elected democratic leader, or install themselves or a military dictator in power.

**Coup d'État:** Trusted generals or associates suddenly lose credibility. Common signs include late-night gunfire near the palace; your chauffeur in a new uniform, nervous bodyguards, and a trusted aide taking his family on vacation far away.

**The Military Coup d'état**

The 1973 Chilean coup d'état is often seen as one of the most important and impactful coups carried out by a military leader turned dictator. It involved the overthrow of democratically elected socialist President Salvador Allende by the Chilean Armed Forces, led by General Augusto Pinochet. The coup led to the creation of a military dictatorship that lasted 17 years.

Pinochet stepped down after losing a 1988 plebiscite, in which 56% of voters rejected his presidency.

**Revolution:** Crowds with torches and slogans louder than your propaganda speakers. Common signs: Protest chants start rhyming with your name—example: Louis XVI — "crowdsourcing" before the internet.

**Elections:** Indira Gandhi's 1977 election loss ended her Emergency, but she returned in 1980 (BBC, 2020). Pinochet's 1988 referendum defeat led to his departure in 1990 (Amnesty International, 2020). Prayut's 2019 Thai elections limited his junta (Amnesty International, 2020).

**Assassinations:** Indira Gandhi was killed on October 31, 1984, in New Delhi while serving her second term in office by two of her bodyguards. Gandhi's 1984 assassination by Sikh bodyguards followed Operation Blue Star (BBC, 2020). Anwar Sadat's 1981 killing highlights the risks of alienating factions (BBC, "Sadat's Death," 2020). Israel's 2024 killing of Ismail Haniyeh ended his Hamas rule (Al Jazeera, 2024).

**Invasion:** U.S. forces removed Saddam Hussein in 2003, leading to his execution in 2006 (BBC, 2003). Muammar Gaddafi's 2011 NATO-backed rebel killing ended his 42-year rule (BBC, "Gaddafi's Fall," 2011).

**Natural Death**: The Dictator of Spain, Franco, died in 1975. aiding Spain's transition to democracy (BBC, 2020). Mao's

1976 death marked the end of China's Cultural Revolution chaos (BBC, 2016).

## DICTATOR DOWNFALLS

| Leader | Exit | Cause | Lesson |
|---|---|---|---|
| Amin | 1979 | Tanzanian invasion | Don't alienate neighbors |
| Marcos | 1986 | People Power uprising | Wealth doesn't stop crowds |
| Ceaușesecu | 1889 | Public revolt | Don't ignore starving citizens |
| Pinochet | 1888 | Election loss | Rig votes better |
| Gaddafi | 2011 | NATO-backed rebels | Avoid foreign enemies |
| Suharto | 1998 | Protests, military pres- | Don't crash the economy |

**Survival Tactics**

**Build Alliances**: Putin's siloviki and Xi's CCP loyalty contrast with Amin's unpredictable purges, which isolated him. Museveni's military connections support him as of 2025 (Human Rights Watch, 2024).

**Control Optics:** Bukele's TikTok charm conceals abuses, unlike Ceaușescu's tone-deaf 1989 speech, which sparked a revolt (BBC, 2020). Pol Pot's secrecy hid genocide but drove away allies (BBC, 2020).

**Plan an Exit:** Marcos took his wealth and fled, unlike Gaddafi, who was killed in a ditch. Guelleh's port wealth secures his family's future in 2025 (Africa Report, 2021).

**Avoid Overreach:** Trump's 2025 legal battles highlight institutional limits, unlike Kim's unchecked rule (CNN, 2025). Suharto's 1998 corruption led to the loss of military support (BBC, 2008).

## Graceful Exits: Plans for the Aspiring Autocrat

As noted earlier, authoritarians cannot imagine ending their dynasties. Nonetheless, immortality and invincibility—regardless of assumptions—are reserved for gods and universal consciousness. Saving for a rainy day and planning for retirement is smart, just in case you need it. A bank account in the Cayman Islands and a private jet hidden somewhere are also worth considering, just to be safe. Your goal is to avoid justice, protect your wealth, rewrite your legacy, and steer clear of those awkward bunker selfies. Here are a few ideas to consider.

### The "Beachfront Villa" Retirement

Flee to a sunny tax haven with no extradition treaties. Bring gold-plated golf clubs, offshore accounts, and a memoir ghostwritten as "My People Loved Me." Study: Marcos in Hawaii (with Imelda's shoe closet as carry-on).
**Key Term:** Palm-frond diplomacy – the art of trading war crimes tribunals for Mai Tai's.

### The "International Lecturer" Route

Rebrand yourself as a global elder statesman. Start giving TED-adjacent talks about "leadership lessons." Earn stacks of speaker fees, smug nodding in Davos panels. Study: Any ex-strongman who suddenly discovers climate change after retirement.

## The "Elder Hermit" Escape

Claim spiritual rebirth, retire to a monastery, write bad poetry. Grow a beard, acquire prayer beads from the Dalai Lama, and a suspiciously large "charitable foundation" trust fund— Study: Diocletian growing cabbages after ruling Rome—only now with Wi-Fi. and Authoritarian Mindfulness—10 steps to ignoring extradition papers.

## The "Friendly Exile" Shuffle

Method: Cozy up to another autocrat who owes you a favor. Spend twilight years as their honored "guest."

A guest house with guards, imported brandy, paranoid insomnia. Study: Idi Amin in Saudi Arabia, living large until the buffet ran out.

**Key Term:** Dictator AirBnB—an international timeshare program for ousted tyrants.

## The "Fake Illness" Strategy

Declare sudden severe illness; disappear to a Swiss clinic with your money in hand. Arrange wheelchair photos, subtle plastic surgery, and a new passport. Study: Francisco Franco—took years to die, but managed to die in bed, not in court or a cell..

## The "Disappear into Business" Maneuver

Shift from politics to running "legitimate" businesses like shipping lines, football teams, and energy monopolies.

Frequent appearances in corporate boardrooms, hiring PR teams, and using logos with suspiciously militaristic fonts. Study: Oligarchs turned "entrepreneurs." Replace statues with billboards, and uniforms with jeans and polo shirts.

**Personal Development:** Practice an "exit speech" blaming "globalists." Mimic Franco's quiet death or Prayut's election pivot to avoid Gaddafi's ditch. Rumors suggest that Vladimir Putin has billions hidden around the world, including, but unverified, property in Switzerland, such as a home registered in someone else's name. It makes you wonder what other authoritarian leaders might have stashed away around the world.

**Conclusion**

Dictatorship 101 works—until it suddenly fails. Nero's fiddle, Gaddafi's desert execution, Ceaușescu's firing squad, and Pol Pot's jungle exile all demonstrate that power fades. By 2025, Orbán faces EU sanctions, Erdoğan battles 70% inflation, Maduro dodges protests, Bukele risks UN investigations, and Bolsonaro's trial approaches with a possible 40-year sentence (Euronews, 2025). Historical failures—Pinochet's referendum, Marcos's exile, Amin's removal, Suharto's fall—highlight the same pattern. Democracy, empathy, and humor last longer than shiny uniforms, TikTok filters, or killing fields. Skip the throne—try improv comedy. The audience is kinder, and there's no guillotine.

**An Ongoing Story: See Chapter 15 for Final Episode.**

*President Paul J Johnston addresses National Conference.*

In the final part of An Ongoing Story, our three recurring characters—Paul S. Johnson, Rob Stevenson, and Margaret Miller—show how authoritarian behavior adapts in politics, business, and personal ambition. Their meeting at the National Renewal Summit highlights the merging of corporate efficiency talk, political spectacle, and opportunistic imitation.

# Chapter 15

## An Ongoing Story Final Episode

*When three rising authoritarians gather under chandeliers and fireworks, each one sees themselves as the star of history's encore. But history shows that only one gets the top spot, while the others wait impatiently for their turn at the podium*

The ballroom at the Capital Grand Hotel shimmered with chandeliers and gold-trimmed banners that read National Renewal. Rows of tables were filled with delegates, donors, and "ordinary citizens," carefully selected by a PR firm's casting call. Cameras scanned the crowd as a booming voice announced: Ladies and gentlemen, please welcome your host — the President of the United States, Paul S. Johnson! Paul stepped onto the stage, illuminated by a spotlight. Behind him, a large screen displayed a live feed of his face, slightly delayed, creating the illusion of a larger-than-life double. The crowd erupted in rehearsed chants: "Paul! Paul! Paul!"

At a table near the front, Senator Rob Stevenson straightened his tie and waved at the cameras. "Not bad," he muttered. "Good practice for when I host my summit."

CEO Margaret Miller sat beside him, perfectly composed. She glanced at the agenda in her hand: Panel on Efficient

Leadership. "They could have just written 'Consolidating Power,'" she whispered dryly.

Rob remembered meeting Margaret Miller at a "Leadership in Democracy" symposium he attended, mainly for the free buffet and to take photos for networking. While waiting in line for coffee, he stood beside a sharply dressed woman talking with a tech investor. Margaret Miller didn't notice him at first—she was explaining how corporate governance could "streamline inefficiency" in a way that sounded suspiciously like executive consolidation. Rob smiled politely. "Hi, I'm Rob Stevenson," he said, handing her his business card. "Hi, good to meet you," she replied, exchanging cards with him. Neither admitted it aloud, but both thought the same thing: a potentially valuable contact. Later, Margaret delivered her keynote on "responsible leadership" to a round of polite applause. Her message was full of language about stability, vision, and trust—classic benevolent authoritarian framing. Watching from the side, Rob observed her poise and thought she could win a city election without even trying.

President Pau S Johnson didn't attend the symposium, but he watched a news segment that showed Margaret's speech and Rob's photo op in the crowd. "Two rising stars," the anchor said. Paul smirked. "More like two future allies... or opponents." He made a mental note to invite both to a "National Renewal" summit—purely for networking, of course.

As CEO, Margaret's position was secure, but she aimed to establish dominance. At the annual shareholders' meeting, she revealed a broad corporate vision called "modernizing for efficiency." It centralized decision-making in her office, leaving just enough ceremonial authority for the board to feel involved. A reporter asked if such extensive central control was risky. Margaret smiled, "Leadership requires courage—and a unified chain of command." The quote made headlines in business circles.

"She's running that company like a mayor runs a city... if the mayor rewrote all the laws," Rob thought. He made a mental note to call her, to "compare strategies," after reading about Margaret's "streamlined corporate governance" in the local paper.

When the news article reached Paul, he saw Margaret's story as political gold. During a rally speech, he praised "strong business leaders who cut through red tape and deliver results." His supporters didn't realize he was talking about Margaret specifically, but the message was clear: he admired her style—and he fully planned to adopt it once in office. She might be someone he could use in his regime.

During a walk in DC, Rob found a "Reference Guide to Popular Authoritarians" at a used bookstore. He quickly studied Orbán, Erdoğan, and Bukele, analyzing their strategies like a coach. "Court stacking, media loyalty, crisis exploitation..." he whispered. At his next Senate committee meeting, Rob proposed creating a "charter clarification" subcommittee— aimed at adjusting rules to his advantage. "But he claimed his goal was just housekeeping," he said, adopting Orbán's tone.

He remembered mentioning it to Margaret Miller during their meeting.

Margaret told him she studied the same guide during her flight to a meeting. She remembered focusing on sections about Xi Jinping's term-limit removal and Atatürk's cultural reforms. She then headed to the next board retreat with a plan: a broad "corporate culture realignment" that subtly reinforced her authority. "It's about legacy," she told her executive team, echoing Xi's carefully chosen words. The board nodded, feeling they were part of something historic—Margaret's story.

Paul S Johnson's Chief of Staff handed him a copy of the book. Paul approached the guide like a playbook. He borrowed Marcos's pageantry, Mussolini's grandstanding, and even a hint of Perón's populism. "Why settle for just rallies," he told his team, "When we can have movements?" His next event featured a coordinated chant, large flags, and a carefully staged photo of him signing "citizen pledges" at a desk—pure political theater that echoed the greats, just updated for social media.

Approval ratings for Senator Rob Stevenson started to decline after a public works project in his state halted and medical insurance benefits were reduced. Critics blamed him for failing to secure the funds, but Rob dismissed these accusations as unfounded. "The numbers are wrong, it's a hoax," he told reporters. "People love me." Behind the scenes, his closest advisor advised caution, but Rob believed that a new state park—featuring a dedication plaque in his name—would solve everything. He didn't realize how quickly allies were abandoning him.

Recently, Margaret's iron grip on the boardroom began to show minor cracks. A shareholder lawsuit accused her of misusing funds in her "corporate culture realignment." Her general counsel recommended a discreet settlement, but Margaret dismissed it. "Settling is weakness. We fight." She intensified her efforts with an aggressive media campaign praising her leadership. It masked the real issue—for now—but dissent in the boardroom was growing louder, even if she refused to acknowledge it. She considered forming alliances with tech billionaires who believed in authoritarian reforms of government.

The new presidential campaign encountered turbulence when a damaging leak revealed questionable campaign funding. Paul's advisors suggested he address it openly. "Never explain, never apologize," Paul snapped. Instead, he hosted an even larger rally, complete with pyrotechnics. The crowd cheered, cameras rolled, and Paul smiled, fully convinced that the spectacle had erased the scandal. Behind the applause, cracks in his support base were beginning to show, but Paul's reflection in the gold-plated stage lights was all he could see. The National Renewal Summit was another chance to dominate the media news cycle.

Leaning toward the podium at the National Renewal Summit, his voice rising with dramatic conviction, Paul said, "Tonight, we unite business, government, and the people in one shared vision—streamlined, decisive, and above all, loyal." He raised his fist as fireworks exploded on a screen behind him, spelling out NATIONAL RENEWAL.

Margaret offered a polite smile to the crowd while quietly observing which CEOs appeared most eager to pledge loyalty. Rob took notes in a small notebook: "Fireworks = applause boost. Maybe use an in-state campaign."

As the crowd cheered, Paul looked around the room and made eye contact with Rob and Margaret. For a moment, he saw not allies but future rivals—each planning their rise, each ready to adopt tactics from the authoritarian playbook.

The summit concluded with standing ovations. Reporters described the event using words like visionary and transformative. Nobody pointed out that every speaker reused the same language — phrases borrowed from past dictators, masked as "renewal."

## Conclusion

This concludes An Ongoing Story. Readers should observe how corporate, political, and personal authoritarian styles merge into a single shared ecosystem. Whether masked by efficiency, loyalty, or renewal, the result remains the same: a continued rehearsal of authoritarianism dressed up as leadership.

This chapter wraps up the serial narrative An Ongoing Story, which has run through the previous chapters. Notice how each character now embodies key authoritarian traits:

Paul refines the display of populist authoritarianism.

Margaret disguises autocracy with the language of corporate reform.

Rob shifts from an ambitious opportunist to an apprentice authoritarian, carefully studying precedents.

Their presence at the National Renewal Summit demonstrates how authoritarian behaviors spread across different areas of influence. For students of authoritarian leadership, this case reminds us that control tactics rarely stay confined to one place. They move, evolve, and reinforce each other—until the rehearsal takes center stage.

*"The whole aim of practical politics is to keep the populace alarmed (and hence clamorous to be led to safety) by menacing it with an endless series of hobgoblins, all of them imaginary".*
*H. L. Mencken*

# *Glossary*

## *Reference Guide to Authoritarian Leaders and Dictators*

This glossary provides brief bios of the listed authoritarian figures, also known as strongmen and hardcore dictators, along with other world leaders, highlighting their rise to power, tactics, and influence. It is not an exhaustive list and isn't meant to be complete. One female authoritarian leader is included since only one of note was found in our search. Additionally, we omitted wannabe or emerging dictators who have not yet established their credentials. It does not include World War II dictators and prior authoritarian leaders in history. Apologies if your favorite dictator was omitted.

**Alexander Lukashenko** (Belarus): President since 1994, Lukashenko, dubbed "Europe's last dictator," seized power in Belarus's post-Soviet chaos, rigging elections and crushing protests, notably in 2020 after his sixth term "win" (BBC, "Belarus Protests," 2020). His Soviet-style tactics—state TV propaganda, jailing opponents like Sviatlana Tsikhanouskaya's team, and loyal security forces—mirror Maduro's playbook. As of 2025, aligned with Putin, he deflects EU sanctions with Russian aid, claiming "stability" while his economy continues to falter.

**Augusto Pinochet** (Chile): Ruler from 1973 to 1990, Pinochet seized power in a U.S.-backed coup against Salvador Allende, establishing a brutal dictatorship (Amnesty International, "Chile's Dictatorship," 2020). His regime killed over 3,000 people and tortured 38,000, using anti-communist fears to justify purges. His 1980 constitution extended his rule, but a 1988 referendum defeat forced his removal. Arrested in 1998, his economic reforms and repression continue to influence Bolsonaro.

**Bashar al-Assad** (Syria): President since 2000, Assad inherited power from his father, Hafez (1971–2000), who had promised reforms as a physician (UN, "Syria Conflict," 2024). The 2011 Arab Spring protests led to his brutal crackdowns, sparking a civil war that has caused over 500,000 deaths. Supported by Russia and Iran, his regime uses chemical weapons and surveillance (OPCW, 2023). As of 2025, Assad controls Damascus but still faces ongoing insurgency.

**Charles de Gaulle** (France): President (1958–1969). During the Algerian War, de Gaulle centralized power and established the Fifth Republic, characterized by a strong presidency (History, "De Gaulle," 2020). His referendums and radio speeches mobilized citizens, but bypassing parliament drew criticism. After losing a 1969 referendum, he resigned, and his democratic restraint contrasts with Xi's lifelong rule.

**Daniel Ortega** (Nicaragua): President (1985–1990, 2007–present). Ortega has transitioned from a Sandinista revolutionary to an autocrat, manipulating elections and imprisoning opponents like Cristiana Chamorro in 2021 (Al Jazeera, "Nicaragua's Crackdown," 2021). His wife, Rosario Murillo, who serves as vice president, helps establish a family dynasty. By 2025, his media bans and protest suppressions resemble Maduro's tactics, yet anti-US rhetoric maintains his support base.

**Ferdinand Marcos** (Philippines): President from 1965 to 1986. Marcos declared martial law in 1972, looting $10 billion while censoring media and jailing opponents

(Amnesty International, "Marcos's Legacy," 2020). His propaganda films and wealth-flaunting rallies projected strength, but the 1986 People Power Revolution ousted him. His son, Ferdinand Jr., won in 2022, reviving the family dynasty.

**Francisco Franco** (Spain): Dictator (1939–1975). Franco won the Spanish Civil War and ruled with Catholic conservatism and brutal purges, killing 50,000 (BBC, "Franco's Spain," 2020). His Valley of the Fallen, built with forced labor, symbolized his reign. His death in 1975 led to Spain's transition to democracy, but his legacy continues to influence far-right nostalgia.

**Getúlio Vargas** (Brazil): President (1930–1945, 1951–1954). Vargas seized power in a 1930 coup and ruled as a populist dictator through the 1937 Estado Novo, combining labor reforms with censorship (BBC, "Vargas," 2020). Ousted in

1945, he returned in 1951 but died by suicide in 1954 amid military pressure.

**Hugo Chávez** (Venezuela): President (1999–2013). Chávez, a former paratrooper, gained prominence after a 1992 coup attempt and won elections driven by oil-funded populism (BBC, "Chávez's Rise," 2002). His Bolivarian Revolution nationalized industries, censored media, and fostered a cult of personality through murals and TV marathons, paving the way for Maduro.

**Idi Amin** (Uganda): Ruler (1971–1979), Amin seized power in a coup, expelled Asians, and purged rivals with erratic brutality, killing up to 500,000 (BBC, "Amin's Reign," 2003). His self-awarded titles, such as "Conqueror of the British Empire," masked chaos. Ousted by Tanzanian forces in 1979, his legacy serves as a warning of megalomania.

**Indira Gandhi** (India): Prime Minister (1966–1977, 1980–1984), Gandhi, Jawaharlal Nehru's daughter, promoted "Garibi Hatao" populism but declared a 1975–1977 Emergency, jailing 140,000 people and censoring the media (BBC, "Gandhi's Emergency," 2020). Ousted in 1977, she returned in 1980 but was assassinated in 1984.

**Ismail Haniyeh** (Hamas, Palestine): Hamas leader from 2006 to 2024. Haniyeh rose through Gaza's Islamist movement and became prime minister after the 2006 elections (Al Jazeera, "Hamas Leadership," 2024). His militant rhetoric and Iranian support fueled conflict, but Israel's 2024 assassination ended his rule, similar to autocrats like Maduro.

**Ismail Omar Guelleh** (Djibouti): President since 1999, Guelleh inherited power from his uncle, using the country's port wealth to stay in control (Africa Report, "Guelleh's Rule," 2021).

His 2021 election results were rigged, rivals were jailed, and internet access was shut down, echoing Maduro's tactics. As of 2025, his strategic port continues to support his grip despite protests.

**Jair Bolsonaro** (Brazil): President from 2019 to 2022. Bolsonaro, an army captain, gained support with anti-corruption and pro-dictatorship rhetoric, using WhatsApp to rally conservatives (Euronews, "Bolsonaro's Rise," 2018). His 2023 coup attempt failed, leading to a trial in 2025 with a potential 40-year sentence (Euronews, 2025).

**Kim Jong-un** (North Korea): Supreme Leader since 2011, Kim inherited power from his father, Kim Jong-il (1994–2011), and grandfather, Kim Il-sung (1948–1994) (BBC, "Kim's Dynasty," 2012). His family tree includes Kim Jong-il's five children: Kim Jong-nam (assassinated 2017), Kim Jong-chul, Kim

Jong-un, Kim Sol-song, and Kim Yo-jong (key advisor). His missile launches and purges help him maintain control.

**Mao Zedong** (China): Chairman (1949–1976). Mao led the Communist Revolution and established the People's Republic (BBC, "Mao's Legacy," 2016). His Great Leap Forward (1958–1962) and Cultural Revolution (1966–1976) caused millions of deaths and enforced loyalty through red books and statues. His cult of personality laid the foundation for Xi.

**Mustafa Kemal Atatürk** (Turkey): President (1923–1938). Atatürk established modern Turkey after the fall of the Ottoman Empire by implementing secular reforms and one-party rule (BBC, "Atatürk's Legacy," 2020). His bans on traditional dress silenced dissent but modernized Turkey, influencing Erdoğan.

**Nayib Bukele** (El Salvador): President since 2019, Bukele, a millennial ex-advertiser, won with TikTok charisma, tackling gangs with 70,000 arrests by 2024 (NPR, "Bukele's Crackdown," 2024). His court stacking enabled a 2024 re-election, but scrutiny from the UN grew as of 2025.

**Nicolás Maduro** (Venezuela): Serving as president since 2013, Maduro, Chávez's successor, solidified power during oil crashes, manipulated the 2024 elections, and banned rivals such as María Corina Machado (New Yorker, 2024). His 90% media control mirrors Lukashenko's, but the emigration of 7 million people weakens his position.

**Paul Kagame** (Rwanda): Serving as president since 2000, Kagame led the RPF to end the 1994 genocide, establishing "stability" through media crackdowns and arresting rivals (Human Rights Watch, "Rwanda's Repression," 2024). His 99% election wins and economic reforms are praised, but opponents face exile.

**Pol Pot** (Cambodia): Khmer Rouge leader from 1975 to 1979, Pol Pot enforced "Year Zero," leading to 1./ million deaths through forced labor and purges (BBC, "Khmer Rouge," 2020). His anti-intellectual stance and secret memorials erased Cambodia's history. After being ousted in 1979, his legacy remains a warning against extremist autocracy.

**Prayut Chan-o-cha** (Thailand): Prime Minister (2014–2023). Prayut led a 2014 coup, promising "Thai values" and stability (Amnesty International, "Thailand's Coup," 2020). His media bans, activist arrests, and bot-driven propaganda echoed Maduro. Elections in 2023 limited his power, but his influence remains.

**Recep Tayyip Erdoğan** (Turkey): Prime Minister (2003–2014) and President (2014–present). Erdoğan shifted from reformer to autocrat after the 2013 Gezi protests, purging 100,000 following the 2016 coup attempt (GMF, "Turkey's Authoritarianism," 2020). His 90% media control continues to fuel unrest as of 2025.

**Robert Mugabe** (Zimbabwe): Prime Minister (1980–1987) and President (1987–2017), Mugabe led Zimbabwe's independence but became autocratic, ignoring experts and causing food crises (BBC, "Mugabe's Fall," 2017). Ousted in a 2017 coup, his land reforms influenced Museveni.

**Rodrigo Duterte** (Philippines): President (2016–2022). Duterte's "war on drugs" killed over 20,000 people, using fear and loyal police (Human Rights Watch, "Duterte's Legacy," 2022). His media harassment silenced Maria Ressa, but term limits forced his departure.

**Saddam Hussein** (Iraq): President (1979–2003).

Saddam rose through Ba'athist ranks, relying on oil wealth and fear (BBC, "Saddam's Image," 2003). His statues, purges, and wars (Iran, Kuwait) demonstrated power, but the U.S. invasion removed him in 2003. He was executed in 2006.

**Kais Saied** (Tunisia): President since 2019, Saied, a law professor, won as an anti-elite outsider, dissolving parliament in 2021 and rewriting the constitution in 2022 (Al Jazeera, "Saied's Power Grab," 2022). His media crackdowns mirror Erdoğan's, but protests in 2025 challenge him.

**Suharto** (Indonesia): President (1967–1998). Suharto took control in a 1965 coup, resulting in the deaths of up to 1 million people in anti-communist purges (BBC, "Suharto's Legacy," 2008). His "New Order" cronyism and media control favored allies, but the 1998 financial crisis ended his rule.

Vladimir Putin (Russia): President (1999–2008, 2012–present). Putin, a former KGB officer, rose to power during the Chechen wars and the chaos of Yeltsin's presidency (BBC, "Putin's Rise," 2020). His shirtless photo ops, RT propaganda, and Navalny's 2021 jailing help him maintain control. His struggles with the Ukraine war in 2025.

**Xi Jinping** (China): President since 2013, Xi rose through the CCP, becoming "Chairman for Life" in 2018 (NYTimes, "Xi's Power," 2018). His Great Firewall, social credit system, and Bo Xilai's purge strengthen his authority. As of 2025, his "Chinese Dream" suppresses dissent.

**Yoweri Museveni** (Uganda): President since 1986, Museveni took power after a civil war, promising stability (Human Rights Watch, "Museveni's Grip," 2024). His 2005 removal of term limits and the 2021 election rigging led to the imprisonment

of Bobi Wine. His control
over the media and military
maintains his rule as of 2025.

*This bibliography lists recommended readings and sources related to the themes, historical figures, and modern examples in \*Dictatorship 101: Guide to Becoming an Authoritarian Leader for Beginners\*. It includes academic works, journalistic reports, and organizational documents to provide a comprehensive understanding of authoritarianism, its strategies, and its effects.*

*The list offers a variety of primary sources, scholarly works, and contemporary analyses to enhance your understanding of the historical aspects of Dictatorship 101. Use these to improve your "leadership" skills— preferably in a comedy club, not during a coup.*

# Bibliography

## Recommended Reading

### General Works on Authoritarianism

Arendt, Hannah. The Origins of Totalitarianism. New York: Harcourt, Brace & Co., 1951.

A fundamental analysis of totalitarian regimes that examines the psychological and political roots of absolute power.

Friedman, Milton, and Rose Friedman. *Free to Choose: A Personal Statement.* New York: Harcourt Brace Jovanovich, 1980.
Provides insights into economic freedom versus authoritarian control, contrasting with the state-driven policies of figures like Chávez.

Levitksy, Steven, and Daniel Ziblatt. How Democracies Die. New York: Crown, 2018. Discusses how leaders like Orbán and relevant to several chapters.

Snyder, Timothy. *On Tyranny: Twenty Lessons from the Twentieth Century*. New York: Tim Duggan Books, 2017.
Provides historical lessons on resisting authoritarianism, pertinent to Chapters 8 and 11.

## Historical Case Studies

Applebaum, Anne. Gulag: A History. New York: Doubleday, 2003.
Details Stalin's purges and labor camps, providing context for chapters 2, 7, and 13.

Beavor, Antony. The Second World War. New York: Wiedenfeld & Nicolson, 2012. Covers Hitler's and Mussolini's wartime strategies, relevant to Chapters 3 and 5.

Chandler, David P. *A History of Cambodia*. Boulder: Westview Press, 2008.
Explores Pol Pot's Khmer Rouge regime, which is central to chapters 1, 2, and 16.

Preston, Paul. Franco: A Biography. New York: HarperCollins, 1993.
A comprehensive biography of Franco's rule, covering chapters 2, 9, and 14.

Short, Philip. Mao: A Life. New York: Henry Holt, 1999.
Details Mao's rise and the Cultural Revolution, which are important for Chapters 6, 7, and 13.

## Modern Authoritarian Leaders

McCoy, Alfred W. Closer Than Brothers: Manhood at the Philippine Military Academy. New Haven: Yale University Press, 1999.

Provides background on Marcos's military roots, informing Chapters 3 and 16.

Naím, Moisés. The End of Power: From Boardrooms to Battlefields and Churches to States, Why Being In Charge Isn't What It Used to Be. New York: Basic Books, 2013.
Discusses modern power dynamics, including Bukele and Maduro, relevant to Chapter 15.

Wong, Edward. China's Great Leap: The Beijing Olympics and the Communist Party's Coming-of-Age. New York: Times Books, 2008.
Examines Xi's rise and China's global image, which are key themes in Chapters 10 and 13.

**Regional Perspectives**

Anderson, Benedict. Imagined Communities: Reflections on the Origin and Spread of Nationalism. London: Verso, 1983.
Explores nationalism's role in leaders like Atatürk and Museveni, relevant to Chapters 3 and 9.

Ellis, Stephen. The Mask of Anarchy: The Destruction of Liberia and the Religious Dimension of an African Civil War. New York: NYU Press, 1999.
Offers context about African dictators like Amin, supporting chapters 1 and 15.

Vatikiotis, Michael R. J. Indonesian Politics Under Suharto: The Rise and Fall of the New Order. London: Routledge, 1998.

Details Suharto's regime, which is central to Chapters 4, 6, and 15.

Yergin, Daniel. The Prize: The Epic Quest for Oil, Money & Power. New York: Simon & Schuster, 1991.

Covers oil's role in Saddam's and Chávez's rule, relevant to Chapters 3 and 7.

## Cultural Commentary and Satire

Frankfurt, Harry G. On Bullshit, Princeton University Press, 2005 A philosophical and satirical examination of the phenomenon once known as "Humbug."

Orwell, George. *Animal Farm*. London: Secker and Warburg, 1945. A satirical allegory of authoritarianism, paralleling chapters 5 and 7.

Vonnegut, Kurt. Mother Night. New York: Harper & Row, 1961. Explores themes of propaganda and identity, offering a satirical perspective in Chapter 7.

Waugh, Evelyn. *Scoop*. London: Chapman & Hall, 1938. A humorous perspective on media manipulation related to Chapter 10.

## Reports and Articles

Amnesty International. "Chile: The Legacy of Augusto Pinochet." 2020.

Details Pinochet's human rights abuses, as presented in Chapters 1 and 8.

BBC News. "Amin's Reign of Fear." 2003.
Chronicles Idi Amin's rule, key to Chapters 2 and 14.

Human Rights Watch. "Museveni's Grip on Power." 2024.
Analyzes Museveni's tactics relevant to Chapters 4 and 15.

NPR. "Bukele's Crackdown on Gangs." 2024.
Covers Bukele's arrests and media strategy, which are central to Chapters 1 and 10.

New Yorker. "Venezuela's Collapse Under Maduro." 2024.
Examines Maduro's economic and political control, informing Chapters 7 and 15.

**Online Resources**

Al Jazeera. "Saied's Power Grab in Tunisia." 2022.
Details Saied's constitutional changes related to Chapters 4 and 15.

Euronews. "Bolsonaro's Rise and Trial." 2025.
Covers Bolsonaro's campaign and legal challenges, which are essential to Chapters 3 and 12.

UN. "Syria Conflict Update." 2024.
Provides data on Assad's war, informing Chapters 1 and 10.

www.ingramcontent.com/pod-product-compliance
Lightning Source LLC
Chambersburg PA
CBHW071309130626
46556CB00004B/1540